Better Homes & Gardens

celebrate the
SEASON
2018

contents

fall

6 As the year morphs into a season of color and thanksgiving, let its beauty inspire your decorating and get-togethers. This chapter, devoted to autumn, assists. Create projects for your home using wood veneer, snippets of ribbon in seasonal tones, and more.

trims

34 Trimming the tree is a tradition unlike any other. Make memorable decorations to trim your evergreen beautifully. Then explore dozens of projects to transform your home—inside and out—into a welcoming wonderland for guests.

food

90 Be prepared for holiday gatherings with these incredible recipes. This kitchen-tested collection offers suggestions for drinks and small plates as well as main courses, sides, and glorious desserts. You'll feel like Santa himself serving smile-evoking sensations!

gifts

120 Surprise everyone on your gift list with handmade presents. Just knowing that you spent time to create a gift makes it more meaningful to the recipient. This chapter offers fun-to-make gift options for all ages. And when it's time to wrap them up—we have you covered!

kids

140 Who would guess that simple supplies—straws, crayons, and beads—could make such beautiful holiday decorations? Kids will love using them to make holiday decorations and gifts. What a joy to spend time together during the season of giving.

in a twinkling

Make clever trims that whip up easy-peasy!

32 autumn glow

88 flip your lid

118 quick & easy appetizers

138 puttin' on the ritz

152 drinking straw ta-da

patterns pages 152–158   **index** pages 159–160   **photography credits** page 160

Better Homes & Gardens

celebrate the SEASON 2018

MEREDITH CONSUMER MARKETING
Consumer Marketing Product Director: Heather Sorensen
Consumer Marketing Product Manager: Tami Perkins
Consumer Products Marketing Manager: Wendy Merical
Business Manager: Diane Umland
Senior Production Manager: Al Rodruck

WATERBURY PUBLICATIONS, INC.
Editorial Director: Lisa Kingsley
Creative Director: Ken Carlson
Associate Editors: Tricia Bergman, Mary Jo Plutt
Associate Design Director: Doug Samuelson
Production Assistant: Mindy Samuelson
Contributing Editor: Sue Banker
Contributing Copy Editor: M. Peg Smith
Contributing Proofreader: Terri Fredrickson

BETTER HOMES & GARDENS® MAGAZINE
Editor in Chief: Stephen Orr
Executive Editor: Oma Blaise Ford
Managing Editor: Gregory H. Kayko
Creative Director: Jennifer D. Madara
Senior Deputy Editor, Food and Entertaining: Nancy Wall Hopkins

MEREDITH NATIONAL MEDIA GROUP
President: Tom Harty

MEREDITH CORPORATION
Chairman and Chief Executive Officer: Stephen M. Lacy

In Memoriam: E.T. Meredith III (1933–2003)

In the Spirit of Christmas

Last December, my daughter and I met my niece and her two children at the Mall of America. Those little sweeties, ages 2 and 5, were in awe of the glistening decorations, yet in reality, a bit overwhelmed by the fast-paced holiday hubbub.

Midway through the afternoon, as their little legs grew weary, something extraordinary happened. A woman from the crowd walked up to my niece, said "Merry Christmas," and handed her tickets for her kids to enjoy the amusement park right there in the heart of the mall. This random act of kindness was a very merry surprise and such a fitting gesture during the wondrous season of giving.

That get-together was magical and memory-making in so many ways. Sharing time with family is truly what brings me the most joy. And seeing the smiles on those kids' faces as they swirled on rides, hands in the air, was certainly an unforgettable image from that blissful weekend.

That's what *Better Homes & Gardens Celebrate the Season* is all about. We show you ways to surprise and delight those you love. You'll discover tasty recipes to share at gatherings and to deliver to friends and neighbors. You'll fall in love with the dozens of incredible DIY decorating projects and inspiration to make your home sparkle. And the gift ideas—there are so many! You'll find pure delight in crafting and baking incredible expressions of joy for everyone on your gift list.

Whether your gift is for family and friends or a random stranger in the crowd, *Celebrate the Season* shares the warmth, love, and generosity of the season. Let's all pass it along.

May the spirit of the season forever fill your heart and home,

Sue Banker

fall

EARTHY AND WELCOMING
Embrace the rich colors of the
season with inviting accessories
for your home.

Beribboned Beauty

Snippets of colorful patterned and solid ribbons nudge
everyday items into seasonal sensations.

FALL FAVORS

A double layer of ribbon, tied into a bow, transforms a paper
cup into a gift holder for bagged treats. Hot-glue the bow
just below the rim and add a handwritten craft paper tag to
complete the gift.

BANDED CANDLE

Wrap a pillar candle with ribbon to band it with seasonal
color. Choose a coordinating narrow ribbon and tack the
layered ribbons to the candle using upholstery tacks, spaced
approximately 1 inch apart.

DETAILED PUMPKIN

A wooden bun furniture foot in a basic pumpkin shape makes a suitable starter for a fall trim. Cut four lengths from each of two colors of ribbon to fit from the top screw to the center bottom as shown; hot-glue the ends in place. Wrap the screw with jute string, tacking in place with hot glue. Choose one of the ribbons and cut four 3-inch long pieces; hot-glue the ends together. Align the loops with the matching ribbons and glue around the stem.

GETTING EDGY

Woven ribbons lend lovely detail to solid-color place mats. Use iron-on binding to hold the ribbons in place, securing the ends to the back.

WALL FLOWERS

Create a long-lasting bouquet from wire-edged ribbons and assorted buttons. For the base, gather a bundle of sticks and tie together with narrow ribbon. To make flowers from short pieces of ribbon, hold one end of a wire while gathering the ribbon on that side. Twist the wire ends together to secure the gathers. To use nonwired ribbon, use a needle and thread and sew running stitches along one side; pull thread to gather ribbon along edge and sew the short ends together. Layer gathered ribbons if you like and sew a button in the center. For leaves, make large ribbon loops then tie cut ends together with narrow ribbon. Hot-glue the ribbon flowers and leaves to stick bundle.

Wood Tones

Veneer brings rich tones to autumn decorating. A sharp crafts knife helps cut fine thin wood sheets with ease.

SEASONAL SIGHT

A single leaf motif captures the essence of the season. Trace the leaf pattern from page 152 onto the back of 5×7-inch light veneer. Place the veneer on a cutting board and carefully cut out the leaf shape using a crafts knife. Place the light veneer on 5×7-inch dark veneer. Insert the veneer layers into an autumn-tone photo frame.

LETTER PERFECT

Flat wood letters are easy to cover with veneer. Crafts stores offer a variety of letter choices in chipboard, wood, plastic, and pressed wood. Use glue appropriate for bonding wood sheets to each letter then clamp the pieces while drying or press with a heavy book or other item. When glue is dry, carefully cut away excess veneer using a sharp crafts knife. For leaves, cut small leaf shapes then lightly score tip to tip; gently bend along score line. Using the photo to guide placement, accent each letter with wood beads and leaves.

WOVEN FAVOR CUP

Meet a little favor that makes big impact during the season of thanks. To make the mini basket, cut ten 3-inch lengths of 1-inch-wide light-wood adhesive-backed veneer banding. Cut three 11-inch lengths of 1-inch-wide dark-wood veneer banding. Weave the veneer strips together; heat-set the pieces together following the veneer manufacturer's directions. Drill three equally spaced holes on each end of the woven strip as shown in the photograph. Overlap the short ends of the strip, aligning holes. Use brads to connect the woven strip into a ring. Place the ring on a 3-inch wood disc and hot-glue the ring to the base on the inside of the ring.

WOODSY WRAP

A wide band of veneer cloaks a plain glass vessel with autumnal warmth. With the grain running vertically, cut a strip of veneer to fit the vase. Woodgrain or unusual markings in the wood sheet add interest to the vase accent. Use strong, clear double-sided tape to adhere the veneer to the vessel.

HANDSOME MAT

Weave together strips of rich grain wood, narrow and wide, to make a handsome place mat or table runner. From veneer banding, cut as many wide and narrow strips as needed to make the desired size mat. Weave the veneer strips; heat-set the pieces together following the veneer manufacturer's directions. Cut a piece of felt slightly smaller than the mat; glue felt to the back of the mat.

NIFTY NAPKIN RING

Make a showy statement at the dinner table with a veneer-embellished napkin ring. Trim a wood napkin ring with a band of veneer topped with a ¾-inch square turned on point. A showy upholstery tack tops the clever ring. To adhere it, snip off the nail from the tack and hot-glue the head onto the square.

DESIGNER DINING

Step up an autumn dinner with showy place settings. Use the pattern on page 152 to cut out acorn pieces from veneer, using a sharp crafts knife and a cutting board. Use masking tape to join the acorn top to the bottom on the back side. Place the oversize acorn between a clear glass dinner plate and a plate charger.

A GOOD FIT

Blocks of various wood tones bring modern elegance to a plain wood tray. Start the design by cutting a piece of veneer to fit a corner. To cut veneer, place it on a cutting board and trim to size using a sharp crafts knife. Continue cutting veneer pieces—large, small, and in various tones—to fit the tray, leaving narrow borders between. Brush wood glue onto each piece and press into place. Lay a sheet of waxed paper over the tray and weight with books until glue is dry.

Go Wild

Bring autumn decor to life with irresistible woodland creatures made with felt, fabric, and natural materials.

WOODLAND FRIENDS

A pair of timid foxes peeks out from this yarn-covered wreath, rich in cozy detail. Each felted wool fox boasts a busy chenille-stem tail and mounts on a skewer to hold it firmly in place. Moss, glittered artificial mushrooms, and a painted snowflake on a wood slice round out backwoods details.

WHAT YOU NEED

White paper
Pencil
Scissors
9×12-inch piece of felted wool in rust, ivory, and rust plaid
Dressmakers chalk
Polyester fiberfill
Fabric glue
Two ¼-inch-diameter black pom-poms
Four ¼-inch-diameter black buttons
Green embroidery floss
Embroidery needle
Sewing thread in rust and ivory
Grey-and-black jumbo chenille stem
Needle-nose pliers
Two 1×8-inch strips of green plaid felted wool
9-inch foam wreath
Yarn in gray and white
Crafts glue
Artists paintbrushes
3 wired spun-cotton mushrooms: 1¾-inch-tall cream, 1¼-inch-tall red, ¾-inch-tall green
Clear glass glitter
Drill and ⅛-inch bit
Transfer paper
1½-inch-diameter round wood slice
White acrylic paint
2 bamboo skewers
Hot-glue gun and glue sticks
Floral moss
Clear mica flakes
5½ yards of 1½-inch-wide green stripe ribbon
6-inch length of ½-inch-wide twill ribbon

WHAT YOU DO

1. Trace patterns, page 153, onto white paper; cut out. Cut a 5×6-inch piece of rust wool and fold in half to measure 2½×3 inches; use dressmakers chalk to trace the fox head onto the doubled fabric. Sew on traced line. Cut out head, adding a scant ⅛-inch seam allowance. Cut a ½-inch-long vertical slit in the center back of the head; fill with polyester fiberfill, then whipstitch the opening closed.

2. Trace the face twice onto ivory felted wool; cut out. Use fabric glue to adhere the face pieces to the head, aligning the straight face edges with the jawlines of the head and abutting the narrow ends of face pieces at the nose point. Glue a pom-pom to the nose. Using green embroidery floss, stitch a black button to each face piece through the layers.

3. Repeat to make a second head using rust plaid felted wool.

4. Trace two body pieces onto rust felted wool; cut out. Trace one chest piece onto ivory felted wool; cut out. Using rust sewing thread and a ¼-inch seam allowance, sew body pieces together along top neck seam. Sew chest piece to body pieces along the chest side edges with ivory sewing thread. Sew body back seam. Clip and turn body. Sew a gathering stitch around the open edge of body. Firmly stuff the body and pull threads to tightly gather. Repeat to make a second fox body using rust plaid felted wool.

5. Whipstitch the back of a fox head to a matching body at top of neck. To make the tail, cut a 4-inch length from jumbo chenille stem. Use needle-nose pliers to tightly bend over the tip on one end. Use fabric glue to secure the unbent chenille stem end into the gathered bottom of the fox body; let dry. Bend the tail around the body as desired. Fringe the ends of a 1×8-inch green felted wool strip and tie around the fox's neck. Repeat the steps to assemble second fox.

6. Wrap gray and white yarn together around the foam wreath to cover completely.

7. Brush a small amount of crafts glue onto each mushroom and sprinkle with glass glitter; let dry.

8. Drill a ⅛-inch-diameter hole near edge of the wood slice. Trace snowflake pattern on page 153 onto paper. Lay transfer paper and pattern on wood slice. Trace over pattern. Paint the snowflake white. Dip the tip of the brush handle into white to paint the pattern dots. Let dry.

9. On the inside bottom of wreath, drill two holes approximately 2 inches apart and halfway into the wreath. Cut two 3-inch lengths of bamboo skewer, making sure each length has one pointed end. Hot-glue a skewer piece into each hole, pointed end up.

10. Drill another hole, centered 1 inch in front of previous holes. Position a fox at top of each skewer, add a dab of hot glue to the bottom of each fox, and push each fox onto the skewer until it sits on the wreath. Trim mushroom wires to 2 inches long. Gather mushroom stems. Thread a clump of floral moss onto the wires and hot-glue the wire stems into the hole. Hot-glue more moss around the mushrooms and foxes. Brush crafts glue on the moss near the foxes, sprinkle with mica flakes, and let dry.

11. Cut a 30-inch and a 32-inch length of 1½-inch-wide green stripe ribbon. Loop the 30-inch piece around the top of the wreath; knot and trim ribbon ends to make a hanging loop. Loop the 32-inch ribbon back and forth to make a 9½-inch-wide bow. Thread 6-inch twill ribbon through the wood slice hole and tie the ribbon around the center of the green stripe bow; trim ends. Hot-glue the bow to top of wreath.

GIVE A HOOT

Whoooo wouldn't love a set of these fun pinecone owls decked out in fine felt details? Each little owl can be made any way you wish. Choose plain wide eyes, bushy eyebrows, or a pointed crown, then layer the wings and add spots if you like.

WHAT YOU NEED

Paper, pencil, scissors
White paper
Felt in ivory, teal, gray, gold, brown, and/or black
Crafts glue
3-inch-tall pinecone
Hot-glue gun and glue sticks

WHAT YOU DO

1. Trace patterns, page 153, onto white paper; cut out. Trace each shape onto appropriate color of felt. Cut out shapes on traced lines.

2. Referring to placement diagrams, page 153, layer and glue two irises and two pupils onto eye background. If desired, add crown or eyebrows above eyes. Hot-glue eyes to narrow end of pinecone.

3. Layer and glue inner wing to outer wing, or use outer wing alone. If desired, glue three spots to wing. Repeat to make a matching wing. Hot-glue wings to pinecone sides.

SO SQUIRRELY

What could be cuter than this fall-theme trivet cover! Using the patterns on page 154, cut the squirrel, acorn, and trivet shapes from felt colors of your choice. Stitch the squirrel and acorn onto a large felt piece. Fold and stitch the piece on two sides to create a darling trivet cover.

Precious Metals

Get royal style on a pauper's budget by turning everything you touch to gold—using easy (and inexpensive) metallic leafing and rubs.

SEE THE LIGHT

Highlight a lamp's textural details with metallic wax. Apply the wax to a clean, dry surface with a paintbrush, then gently buff with a lint-free cloth to a lustrous finish. When the wax is cured, spray the entire surface with clear acrylic-base varnish.
NOTE: Metallic wax works on most surfaces and doesn't require primer. High shine surfaces might need sanding first.

TAKE A SEAT

Embellish any flat surface, like a chairback, with an intricate gold-leaf pattern. Pick a stencil or draw a pattern if you feel artsy. Spray adhesive on the back of the stencil, let it dry to tacky, then set it in place. Using a foam pouncer, apply liquid leaf over the stencil, let dry, and cover the design with leaf sealer to protect it.

GUARD IT

The newly gilded curlicues of this mirror will age well thanks to a protective coating. Sealing projects makes the leaf durable for years, protecting against flaking and damage from handling and dust. Apply two light coats of spray sealer, allowing to cure fully between coats and before handling the piece. The metal finish will dull slightly after it is sealed. A few coats of gold spray paint tie home decor accents, like this dinosaur, into his metallic surroundings.

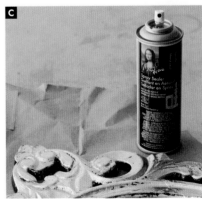

MIXED METALS

Turn an ordinary vase into a modern masterpiece using dramatic swishes of several metallic finishes. Use gold, copper, and silver leaf foil sheets to create the design. For basic leafing directions, see below.

HOW TO APPLY METAL LEAF

WHAT YOU NEED
Plain vase
Lint-free cloth
Metal-leaf adhesive
2 foam brushes or paintbrushes
Sheets of metal leaf

NOTE: Metal leaf is a micro-thin sheet of metal. Imitation leaf is more affordable and easier to use than leaf made from precious metals.

WHAT TO DO
1. Prepare the surface by wiping away dust with a lint-free cloth. Apply a thin coat of leaf adhesive to the entire surface using a foam brush or a paintbrush as shown in Photo A, opposite. Let stand about 30 minutes, or until surface is tacky and the glue changes from white to transparent.
2. Use tissue paper backing to carefully lay foil sheets over the glued areas and gently rub them into place with a clean, dry foam brush or paintbrush, as shown in Photo B. Continue until the surface is covered, overlapping sheets if needed.

3. After the glue dries, use a clean foam brush or dry paintbrush to gently remove excess flakes. A cracked, antique look is desired.
4. To finish, spray the entire surface with sealer, as shown in Photo C and let it dry.

Seasonal Tributes

Celebrate autumn inside and out by displaying pumpkins, gourds, and leaves everywhere.

ARTISTIC PUMPKINS

Observe the harvest season by lightly carving delightful fall foliage designs into a medley of pumpkins for your front stoop or autumn table. For inspiration, check out autumn silhouette images online.

FALL DECOR

A minimalistic autumn landscape, captured under glass, creates a showstopping display. In a container that has a base and domed glass lid, arrange a mound of moss, a leafy twig, and mini gourds.

GATHER 'ROUND

A white pumpkin, insides scooped out to make room for a small vase of flowers, is a serene autumn centerpiece. Prop it on a slice of wood, bark intact. Succulents and metallic candleholders add to the dramatic and stylish tabletop.

METAL MAGIC

Votive candleholders add a golden glow to the tablescape. To make a candleholder, clean the inside and outside of the glass. Cover your work surface. Spray a light mist of water into a glass candleholder, as shown in Photo A. Working inside the candleholder, spray a light layer of metallic gold paint over the beads of water, leaving the glass slightly translucent. Let dry. Spray the interior of the candleholder with gold glitter spray paint, as shown in Photo B. Let dry.

Autumn Glow

BLOSSOMING SHADOWS

Black lace enhances votive candleholders to create romantic silhouettes. Cut lace pieces to fit the candleholder. Brush decoupage medium onto the back of lace pieces and press into place. Once dry, remove excess decoupage medium using a sharp crafts knife.

NATURAL ARRANGEMENT

Squatty gourds make unexpected taper candleholders. Trace the candle base onto the gourd; cut out using a crafts knife. Insert the tapers, wedging with toothpicks for stability if needed.

LIGHT THE WAY

Swirls of alcohol ink add artistic appeal to plain pillar candles. Squirt ink onto waxed paper. Roll a candle in the ink until covered. Ink the top with a felt applicator or brush. Starting at the rim, drip different colors of ink—as well as a metallic blend—onto the candle exterior, as shown in Photo A. Drip on blending solution to help spread the metallic. Spritz alcohol to further marble the applied colors. Let dry 24 hours before use.

LAST-MINUTE SUPERSTAR

Cabbage leaves accent plain glass votive candleholders. Set a candleholder on a leaf, fold the leaf upward, and secure it with string tied in a bow.

trims

From cozy country to glittery glam, this chapter offers wondrous inspiration to express holiday style.

For the Love of Lodge

Delight in making easy-to-do trims that are both casual and festive.

NATURE-INSPIRED ORNAMENTS

Animal-shape cookie cutters set the stage for these quaint ornaments. To make the shapes stand out on the tree, use pinking shears to trim stiffened felt pieces ¼ inch beyond cutter edges. Stitch felt backing to cookie cutter using embroidery floss. If felt is difficult to sew through, use an awl to poke holes along edges of cookie cutters before stitching. Stitch a French-knot eye for each animal. Stitch a loop through felt edge for ornament hanger.

GRAND FOCAL POINT

A pair of stiffened gray felt floor mats are the "fabric" for this oversize wall stocking. Fill with artificial or fresh greenery for a striking holiday decoration. Draw a 20×30-inch stocking shape onto newspaper using the mats as a size guide. Use the pattern to cut two shapes from stiffened felt; cut out shapes. Use a ruler to mark every inch around the edge on one stocking shape. Align the felt pieces atop each other. Place a wood scrap under the stocking edge where marked. Use a ⅛-inch bit and drill through each marking, drilling through both layers. Using blanket stitches (see diagram, page 158) and red yarn, stitch the stocking layers together. Cut an 8×14-inch piece of faux fur for cuff; hot-glue to top of stocking. In lieu of buttons, use three lids such as the ends from frozen juice cans or biscuits. Use an awl to puncture four holes through each lid, as indicated below, then stitch an X on each using yarn. Hot-glue the buttons to the stocking as shown.

MERRY MITTEN

Create mini mittens just the right size to hold silverware, hide gift cards, or hang on the tree. Use the pattern on page 152 and pinking shears or straight-edge scissors to cut two mitten shapes from stiffened felt, three 1-inch-diameter circles, a ¾×3-inch cuff, and a ½×3-inch strip for bow. Use long stitches to sew the cuff to the right side of the mitten. Sew a disk bead to each felt circle; hot-glue to mitten front. Use running stitches to secure mitten front to back. Tie the strip in a knot; trim ends to make a bow shape. Hot-glue the bow to the right side of the mitten cuff; add a hanging loop if desired.

TREE-TRIMMED TABLERUNNER

A pretty woolen plaid scarf adds a warm touch to the tabletop. For embellishment, cut four felt trees, using the pattern on page 152. Attach two trees to each end of the scarf, using running stitches along the center of each tree.

SEW SIMPLE BASKET LINER

Sew simple, so cute! With a few handmade accents, a plain linen
napkin makes a cheery basket liner. Use embroidery floss to edge
the napkin with blanket stitches. Back a coordinating decorative
pin with a felt circle and trim a narrow border. Outline the edge with
running stitches. Pin the decoration to one corner of the napkin.

SNOW BUDDIES

Made from plastic light globes, these frosty friends bring big smiles to indoor spaces.
Hot-glue a smaller globe to the top of a larger one. In a well-ventilated work area,
spray-paint the globes white and let dry. Spray on a second coat and let dry. To add
shading, mist the lower part of each globe with light blue spray paint; let dry. Use hot
glue to attach button eyes and mouth. Paint a button form red for the nose; let dry. Hot-
glue the nose in place. Brush white acrylic paint on the top of each button to resemble
snow. Use fleece to make a scarf, fringing the ends. For fleece hat, cut a strip long
enough to wrap around globe and extending 6 inches at the top. Sew the short ends of
the strip together to form a ring. Use embroidery floss to stitch one edge with blanket
stitches; turn up for brim. Place hat on snowman. Wrap hat top with embroidery floss
and secure.

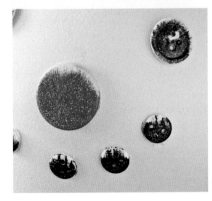

WINTER-CHARMED COCOA MUG

Spread holiday cheer by giving mugs filled with hot chocolate mix in a bow-tied bag. To make the mix more festive, sprinkle the top of the mix with crushed candy canes and marshmallows.

CHEERFUL TABLETOP EVERGREEN

A simple seedling becomes sensational with adornments blanketing the planter and branches. Add a scrapbook embellishment to the planter that shares a seasonal message. Tie the pot with a generous ribbon bow dotted with a holiday button. Wire lightweight miniature ornaments to the branches and add a second holiday button for the topper.

Trims

BIG STITCH COASTERS

Simple blanket stitches edge stiffened felt for make-quick coasters. For each coaster, cut a 5-inch square of felt. Using a ruler, make a mark every ½ inch, ½ inch in from the edge. Place the felt square on a cutting board. Use an awl to poke holes where marked. Finish the edge with contrasting yarn blanket stitches.

RUSTIC CHARM PILLOW

Personalize a plaid pillow with DIY buttons made from branch slices. Drill two ⅛-inch holes in the center of each slice. Sew them onto a plaid pillow cover in the desired simple shape (monogram, tree, candy cane) using an embroidery needle and jute string.

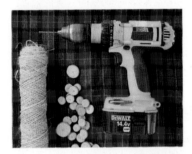

RING TONE

This striking oversize wreath is made with unlikely materials—hula hoops!
A douse of metallic copper spray paint gives the plastic surfaces of a
small and large hula hoop luxurious sheen. Use copper wire to hold the
hoops together, then add an asymmetrical arrangement of greens,
dried florals, and a bow over the wired portion.

Pretty as a Poinsettia

Heed the flower of the season to inspire art pieces and decorative accents.

ARTISTIC BLOOM

Melted crayon "paint" and black ink combine for rich batik appeal.

WHAT YOU NEED

Crayons in yellow, orange, red, pink,
 light green, and dark green
Paper cupcake liners
Cupcake tin
Jellyroll baking pan
Waxed paper
10-inch square of cotton fabric
Paintbrushes
Black food coloring
Paper towels

WHAT YOU DO

1. Break a crayon of each color into separate cupcake liners; place liners in cupcake tin as shown in Photo A. Heat crayons in a 350°F oven (about 10 minutes) until melted.

2. Line the baking pan with waxed paper. Place the cotton fabric square on the waxed paper. Paint yellow and orange dots in the center of the fabric as shown in Photo B.

3. Paint pink and red poinsettia petals around the center, painting an inner ring of pink petals first (Photo C) with red outer petals (Photo D). Allow borders of the white fabric to show between shapes.

4. Paint a few leaf shapes using light green, as shown in Photo E. Using dark green, feather-brush strokes outward from the poinsettia and leaves, allowing white space around each shape, as shown in Photo F. Let the wax dry.

5. Crumple the painted fabric as shown in Photo G, allowing the wax to crack.

6. Flatten the fabric and replace on the waxed paper. Paint the entire poinsettia design with black food coloring, as shown in Photo H. The wax will repel the dye. Dab away any excess dye with paper towels.

7. Mat and frame the poinsettia in a 12-inch square frame.

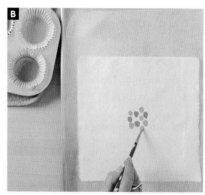

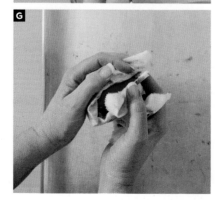

FLOWER FRAME

Edge a photo frame with tinsel trim, add a couple of mini poinsettias, and dust with white acrylic paint for a snowy showy holiday decoration. To complete the look, make an insert of holiday stickers that combine words and images.

FAUX REAL

Nestle lifelike crepe paper poinsettias in bunches on an evergreen swag or add a couple to a vase of greenery for a subtle accent. Use the patterns on page 155 to cut petals and leaves from heavyweight crepe paper. For a more realistic look and more shapable petals and leaves, cut the pieces with the grain running horizontally across the shapes. Glue a piece of wire onto the center back of each one, then gather the pieces, smallest petals centered around a cluster of artificial stamens.

DRESSY NAPKIN RING

So graceful, these napkin rings add festive flair to the table. Make them all one color or vary the color of the napkins to lend variety.

WHAT YOU NEED
Paper cocktail napkins
Hole punch
String
Hot-glue gun and glue sticks
Glitter

WHAT YOU DO
1. Fold napkin from corner to corner in a triangle; repeat twice.
2. Cut around the short sides of the triangle, leaving corners intact so it looks like half a bract. Open and cut apart the four layers.
3. Stack and fan the layers. Fold in half.
4. Make a hole in the bottom center of stack. Thread 6 inches of string through the hole; knot.
5. Pinch and lightly twist the knotted area; open plant.
6. Dab hot glue in open center and sprinkle with glitter; let dry.
7. Tie the poinsettia around a dinner napkin.

HIGH IMPACT

Poinsettia bracts are showstoppers when cut for arrangements. To display them in little glasses, first dab away any sap and burn the ends with a lighter to keep water clear and make them last 2 to 3 days. For an easy centerpiece that stays lush all season, group small potted poinsettias in a shallow bowl.

Seaside Inspiration

Shells, starfish, and messages in a bottle transform into holiday decorations that show a love for the sea.

STAR-TOPPED TREES

Glittered stars add glistening accents to tone-on-tone trees. For each base, cover a papier-mâché cone with white or natural-tone burlap. Fold fabric at bottom to the underside of the cone. Trim off excess burlap and hot-glue in place. Using the photo for inspiration, embellish each tree using shell necklaces or single shells, starfish, and jute bows. For each starfish topper, brush on a coat of decoupage medium and sprinkle with glitter.

WREATH PACKAGE TRIM

A simple ring of shells becomes a mini wreath, naturally. Thread small shells onto wire and shape into a ring; twist wire ends together to secure. To tie shell wreath to a gift bag, fold over the bag top and punch a pair of holes through all layers. Thread ribbon through the holes and tie the wreath onto the bag.

CAROLING CHERUB

Craft heavenly delights to grace tree or top extra-special gifts. Use a scallop shell for the gown. Hot-glue a wood bead to the top for a head. Draw eyes and a mouth with a black marking pen. Wrap the top of the bead with jute; hot-glue in place. Thread a wire with small metallic gold beads to make a halo to fit the bead; glue to the jute hair. Glue two beads to the gown to resemble buttons. Using shear ½-inch-wide ribbon, tie a multiple loop bow slightly wider than shell. Glue bow to the back of the wood bead for wings. Add a hanging loop if desired.

GLAD TIDINGS

Add a heavenly touch to each place at the table. For each place card, use a scallop shell for the gown. Brush it with decoupage medium and sprinkle with glitter. Hot-glue a wood bead to the top for a head and a gold ring for a halo. Using gold ¼-inch-wide ribbon, tie a multiple loop bow wider than shell. Glue bow to the back of the wood bead for wings. Fold 4×3-inch white cardstock, long edges together. Trim the lower edge of the place card front with 1-inch-wide sheer ribbon; wrapping ends to the inside and taping in place. Hot-glue an angel to each place card.

SHIMMER AND GOLD NAPKIN RING

Cut burlap to cover a napkin ring. Fringe the edges and hot-glue burlap to the ring. Wrap the ring twice with jute; knot ends. Hot-glue a glittered starfish to the ring, adding a small jingle bell to the center of the star.

MESSAGE IN A BOTTLE WREATH

Maintain the nautical theme with front-door decor that rivals a wreath of green. Wrap a plastic foam wreath with jute rope; hot-glue in place. Write a pair of holiday messages on paper strips that fit inside plastic bottles. Slip paper in each bottle; hot-glue one end to hold each in place. Knot the ends of three 10-inch pieces of rope; glue to the bottom of the wreath. Hot-glue starfish, bottles, and gold beads to lower portion of the wreath.

OUT ON A LIMB

Gnarled branches offer lots of places to hang holiday ornaments. "Plant" them in a bucket filled with sand; add rocks and shells on top of the sand. Paint a pair of starfish seafoam green; let dry. Hot-glue a hanger to one point of each starfish. Hang the pair in the front of the tree. Fill in the rest of the twig tree with small ball ornaments and shells.

SEA-INSPIRED CENTERPIECE

Accent natural shells with colors from the ocean. Place a pillar candle in the center of a glass candle dish. Fill the dish with sea glass. Using the photograph for inspiration, arrange shells around the candle.

PRETTY PRESENTATION

A large clean shell adds a unique focal point to a serving dish. Place the shell in a pedestal bowl and let little cookies and candies flow out of it for all to enjoy.

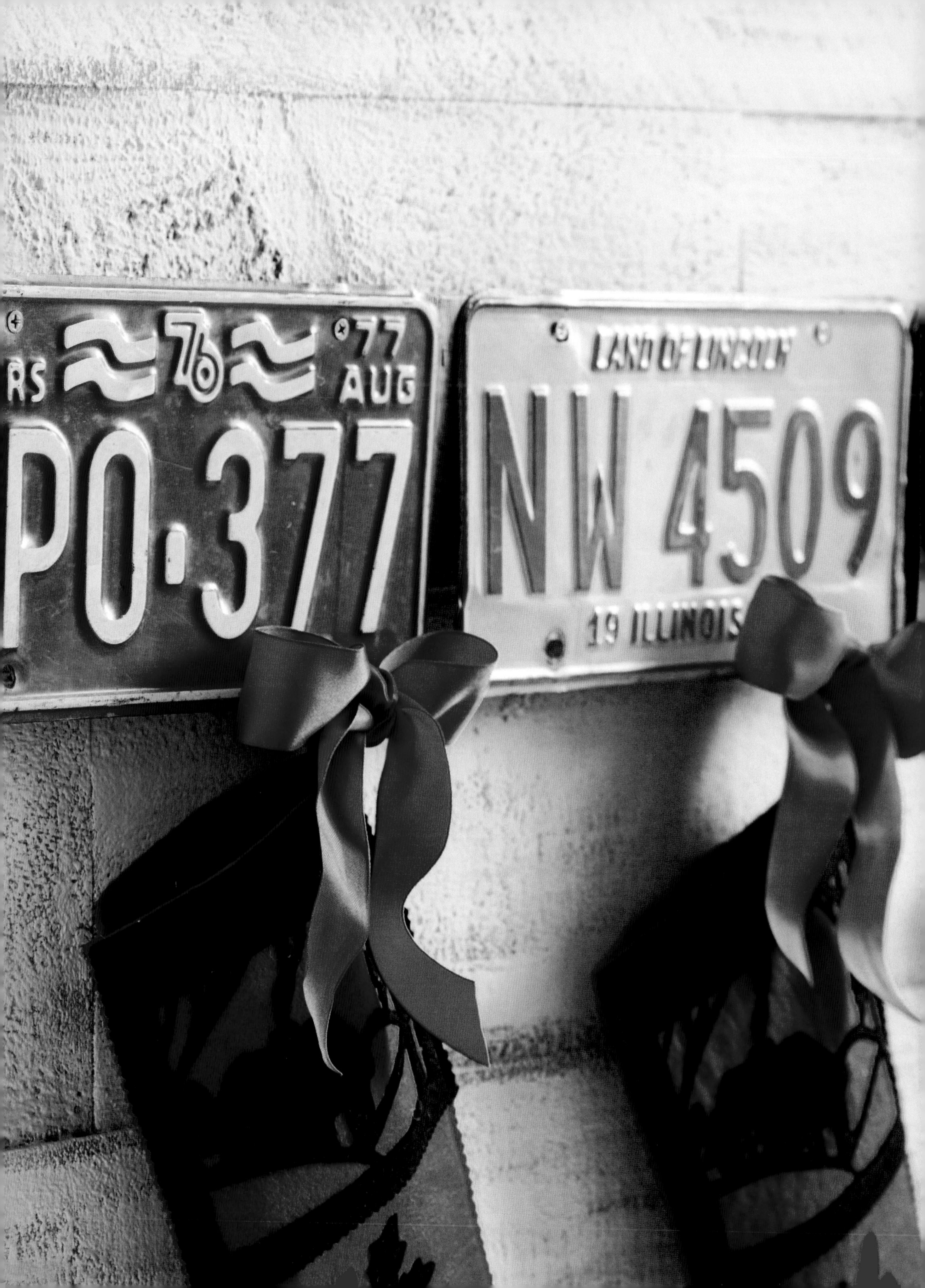
76
77
AUG
PO·377
LAND OF LINCOLN
NW 4509
19 ILLINOIS

Artistic License

Vintage license plates in traditional holiday colors get a magnificent second go-round spreading good cheer throughout your home. When cutting license plates, wear protective gloves and use tin snips to cut. To smooth rough edges, buff the edges with a sanding block.

PEGGED STOCKING HOLDER

Nostalgic charm abounds with a trio of license plates lined up to hold holiday stockings. Cut a board that measures the length of three license plates. Attach the plates to the board using ½-inch wood screws inserted through the mounting holes. Drill through the lower right mounting hole on each license plate. Insert a screw through the back of the wood and through the mounting hole; attach a peg to each screw to hold stockings. Nail sawtooth picture hangers to the back of the board to hang the stocking holder on the wall.

CHRISTMAS CARD CRADLE

Two folds in a license plate create a holiday card holder that's both simple and functional. Use a board or the edge of a work surface to fold over 2 inches from one end of a license plate. Make a second fold 2 inches in from the first. To line the holder, wear protective gloves and use tin snips to cut a piece from a contrasting license plate to fit the inside back. Carefully smooth the cut edge with a sanding block. Wire the license plates together through the mounting holes.

NOSTALGIC NAPKIN RING

A license plate or two can make casual napkin rings for an entire dinner party. For each napkin ring, put on protective gloves and cut a 7×2½-inch piece from a license plate using tin snips; carefully smooth edges with a sanding block. Use a rolling pin to shape the metal strip into a ring; overlap ends slightly.

JAR JACKET

A simple arrangement of holiday greenery becomes extra-special resting in a jar wrapped with a red-and-white license plate. Use a rolling pin to shape the plate into a cylinder and set the jar inside.

PURE FRESH
CANDY

TAG, YOU'RE IT

Bits and pieces of license plates make charming monogram package tags and key chains. Put on protective gloves and carefully cut out the desired area using tin snips. Smooth the edges with a sanding block. Drill a hole at the top and thread with ball chain.

STAR PERFORMER

Use a ruler to draw diagonal lines on the back of three license plates. Put on protective gloves and carefully cut along the lines using tin snips. Smooth the edges of five pieces using a sanding block. Using the photo as a guide, overlap the license plate pieces to form a star shape. Tack the pieces in place using duct tape on the back. Place some metal glue between the shape layers and let dry.

Merry & Bright

Glittery and full of pattern, these holiday decorations sparkle with good cheer.

CHRISTMAS DAY TRIBUTE

Half the fun is in the hunt when it comes to this charming ornament. Search antique stores and flea markets for a license plate bearing a "25." Use a ruler to draw a border around the numbers. Put on protective gloves and carefully cut out the numbers using tin snips. Smooth the edges with a sanding block. Hot-glue red-and-white chenille stem trim around the edge. Drill a hole at the top and thread with leather lacing to hang the ornament.

JOY-FILLED BOX

A sewing machine drawer, dressed up with license plates and pieces, makes a rustic container for a collection of holiday trims. Use star-shape upholstery tacks to attach a small license plate and the letters J, O, and Y to one side.

GRAND HELLO

Welcome holiday guests with an ice skate-embellished wreath decked in playful colors and details. To spruce up the skates, replace the laces with ribbon. Make a yarn pom-pom for each skate and tie a contrasting jingle bell in the center; tie onto the lowest lace. Make multiple ribbon bows for each skate; tie to top laces. Use wire to secure skates to the lower part of an artificial or real wreath. Wire on plastic ornaments, large and small, that blend with the color theme. Top the wreath with a large ribbon bow.

TINY TOWN MANTEL

Festive miniature houses, decked out in whimsical details, create a cheery scene atop the mantel. Bottlebrush trees and big-cuffed stockings complete the wintry wonderland.

HOLIDAY HOUSES

WHAT YOU NEED
Papier-mâché houses
Off-white acrylic paint
Paintbrush
Candle, optional
Tracing paper
Pencil
Scissors
Coordinating scrapbook papers
Decoupage medium, such as Mod Podge
Small-tip glue gun
Glue sticks
Embellishments, such as ribbon, stickers,
    scrapbook trims, buttons, jingle
    bells, faux birds, bottlebrush trees,
    and more
Spray adhesive
Disposable nonlatex gloves, if desired
Glitter

WHAT YOU DO

1. Paint entire papier-mâché house with off-white acrylic craft paint; let dry. Apply a second coat of paint to areas that will not be covered with paper. Allow to completely dry. If, after painted, the top of the house does not slide back on, easily rub a white candle around the edges.

2. Using tracing paper and a pencil, create patterns for areas to be papered, such as roof sections and gables. Label and save patterns for future houses. Select papers and trace around patterns. Then cut out pieces. If using stripes, plaids, or repeated patterns, align patterns so design is maintained when pieces are reassembled.

3. Using a paintbrush, apply decoupage medium to the house. Papering one section at a time, apply the paper piece on glued area.

4. For inside of windows, select paper. Cut squares slightly larger than window opening. Apply decoupage medium to the inside of the window frame. Fasten paper square so color faces out. Use the same technique for the door.

5. Using hot-glue, adhere trim to roof edges and ridges. Fashion ribbons and other embellishments to create a roof topper; attach with hot glue.

6. If using bottle brush trees, select trees for size and color. Remove any wooden or plastic base and, using pliers, bend the center wire so the tree will stand flush on the base of the house. Using thumbs,

separate bristles on one side of the tree to create a wedgelike opening all along the length of the tree. Apply a line of hot glue to the entire length of the opening and around the base of the tree. Quickly press tree into the front corner of the house and hold firmly until glue sets up.

7. If desired, wear disposable gloves while glittering to protect hands. In a well-ventilated work area and working on one side of the house and roof at a time, spray house with adhesive; sprinkle with glitter and let dry.

SUITED FOR SANTA

Soft and sweet, these stockings have personalized trimmings to make each one unique. Use the pattern on page 157 to cut two stocking pieces from soft textured fabric and two lining pieces from cotton fabric. Cut a 16×20-inch cuff from faux fur. With wrong sides facing and using a ½-inch seam, sew the stocking pieces together. Turn the stocking right side out. With right sides facing, sew the lining pieces together using a ½-inch seam. Slip the lining inside the stocking. With right sides and short ends together, sew the cuff into a loop using a ½-inch seam. Fold the cuff piece in half, wrong sides facing. Place the cuff inside the stocking top, aligning raw edges. Sew the cuff to the stocking; fold to the outside. Trim the cuff with embellishments, such as yarn pom-poms, snowflake trims, jingle bells, plastic ornaments, and bows.

BEST-DRESSED GIFTS

Turn your imagination loose while honing your gift-wrapping skills to make lovely tree trims with coordinating papers and trims. Budget-price jewelry boxes are easily transformed into festive tree trims using paper scraps, ribbon snippets, and holiday embellishments of all kinds. Nestle the gift boxes in tree limbs for big impact.

CHARMING CANDLEHOLDER

Cut rectangles and triangles from coordinating holiday scrapbook papers to create basic house shapes to build on. Craft enough houses to cover the surface of a straight-sided glass vessel; adhere houses to vessel using clear double-sided tape. Add window, door, and tree shapes to complete the scene. Use white glue to add glitter "snow" to the tops of shapes.

SNOW FRIENDS

Darling and diminutive, mini snow friends add playfulness to holiday decorating. To make a snowman, hot-glue a glittered plastic foam ball onto a pinecone. Cut the tip off an orange toothpick and glue into the foam ball for the nose. Use short black map pins for eyes. Tie on a ribbon scarf. Top the snowman with a felt hat trimmed with chenille stem and tiny embellishments; glue to head.

POM-POM ORNAMENTS

Inspired by ice skate adornments, these puffs of yarn add softness to tree branches. To make a pom-pom, cut a 4×2½-inch piece a cardboard. Choose two similar colors of yarn. Wrap the yarns around the 2½-inch width of cardboard 50 times. Slide yarn off the cardboard and tightly tie the wraps in the center using a long length of yarn. Thread one yarn end onto a large-eyed needle. Thread a jingle bell onto the yarn; remove needle. Tie the yarn lengths together tightly to secure the jingle bell. Snip the loop ends.

WOODLAND WOW

White owls, twine-tied packages wrapped in plaid and kraft papers, and a burlap skirt ensure that the tree has a rustic woodland vibe.

Cabin Fever

Even if your home isn't nestled in the pines, you can enjoy cabin coziness amid plaid, pinecones, and rekindled spirits.

HUNT AND GATHER

Casual is key for the from-the-woods look of the porch. A garland drapes around the door, cut pine and pinecone branches spill from a bucket, and birch branches lean against the siding. A grapevine wreath with an earthy mix of pinecones, twigs, pods, moss, and nuts—all hot-glued in place—ground the vignette.

STARRING ROLE

Pinecones scooped off the ground (or from a crafts supply store) form a star-shape ornament to use on a tree or package. Hot-glue various sizes of pinecones together to form a star, and adorn the center with a pinecone end cut into a "floret."

NESTING INSTINCT

Herald nature's beauty with a make-in-minutes tabletop accent. Place a bird nest from a crafts supply store filled with jingle bell "eggs" atop faux snow in a clear glass vessel. Perch a faux bird on the nest. Fill in with greenery and berries.

PLAID APLENTY

Plaid is a natural for a cabin-inspired theme, particularly when it stars as a stocking hanging from the mantel. Use old flannel shirts—from a thrift shop—to cut and sew into basic stocking shapes, mixing plaids on stocking front and back if desired. Trim the cuffs with faux fur.

MAIL CALL

Clipped onto ribbon, holiday cards from family and friends become art for everyone to enjoy. Use tape or an adhesive-back strip or hook to attach wide burlap ribbon to the back of a door; then bring the ribbon over the top of the door front. Attach cards using wooden clothespins.

GAME ON

This fun table presentation recalls memories of huddling around the fireplace on a blustery day and playing board games. Lay old Scrabble boards (or a mix of game boards) along the center of a table, spelling out festive words with the game tiles. If desired, adhere the game pieces in place with hot glue or leave them loose for playtime. Fill small jars with the remaining game tiles, strategically placing some facing out to spell a wintry word.

TABLE MANNERS

A burlap runner and an unadorned potted tree wrapped in burlap keep the table setting casual. Game tiles forming guests' initials (or names) serve as place card holders when rested in sawed-to-size wooden holders from old Scrabble games. Green glassware and red napkins bring traditional tones to the display.

Holiday Traditions

It's the most wonderful time of the year! Celebrate with traditional accents that make the holidays bright.

STITCHED FOR ST. NICK

These stockings are sure to be hung with care year after year. Handcrafting them is easy with relaxed yarn stitches and fabric glue. Use the diagrams on page 158 as a guide for adding running, couching, and blanket stitches to the stocking fronts.

FELT TWIRLERS

Handmade ornaments are nostalgia bearers. Unpacking them each year is like discovering pieces of holiday history. Use spray adhesive to join two 9×12-inch felt sheets; cut out two 3½-inch-diameter circles. Cut two 3½-inch-diameter circles from a sheet of iron-on glitter; cut glitter circles in half. Iron glitter half circles to felt circles so one half of each is glitter on the front and other half is glitter on the back. Cut halfway up center of each felt circle (along glitter edge). Slip the two circles together at right angles as shown in photo. Secure cut edges with fabric glue. Cut a 4×6-inch piece of felt and iron-on metallic sheet; iron together. Cut fringe along the 6-inch side, leaving a ¾-inch border across the top. Cut two 24-inch lengths of elastic cord; fold in half. Hot-glue folded ends at one edge of the unfringed top of felt. Starting at that edge, tightly roll felt, dotting with glue as you roll. Knot the loose cords at top of tassel. Thread on beads, knot again. Lay a length of cord in each right angle of twirler; knot at top of ornament and hang.

SPICED COOKIE COTTAGE

Gingerbread houses have inspired family projects since the 1930s. Skip the prefab kit, bake your own cottage, then gather your crew to decorate. If you build it, they will come.

THE BUILDING MATERIALS

The Roof For rooftop shingles, spread melted candy coating in a thick layer on a baking sheet lined with foil. When set, break into shingles and attach with Royal Icing. Instead of melted candy coating, try these: Frosted Mini-Wheats, heart-shape gingersnaps, or Golden Grahams.

The Walk Pave the walk with cobblestone-color jelly beans and a mortar of Royal Icing. Coarse white sugar shimmers like snow alongside it. Instead of jelly beans try these: cocoa nibs, peanut brittle, or Peanut Butter Cheerios.

The Wreath The wreath above the door is a circle of thin twisted rope licorice tied with a ribbon. Brush with gold luster dust for added sparkle. Instead of red rope licorice, try these: milk chocolate medallions, peppermint candies, or green apple gummy rings.

THE DECORATING DETAILS

Windows and Door Use ropes of dough to outline each window and door. After baking, pipe on string lights with icing.

Window Decor Red fruit leather makes colorful curtains. Tie thyme branches together with fine golden twine and attach above windows.

White Planters and Awning Cut out and attach rectangular pieces of dough (included in patterns). Create texture in white Royal Icing using a fork or wooden skewer.

Shrubs Paint rosemary tips with blue Royal Icing. Other herbs like sage and oregano would work too.

SPICED COOKIE DOUGH

You will need two batches, made one at a time. The total amount of dough is more than a mixer can handle at once. Prepare dough at least 2 hours ahead.

WHAT YOU NEED TO MAKE DOUGH

4 cups all-purpose flour, plus 2 tsp.
1 tsp. baking powder
2 tsp. Chai Spice Blend (recipe, right) or
    purchased blend
1 cup butter
1 cup sugar
⅔ cup light-color corn syrup
1 tsp. vanilla
1 egg, beaten

WHAT YOU DO TO MAKE DOUGH

1. In a large bowl combine 4 cups flour, baking powder, and spice blend; set aside.
2. In a medium saucepan combine butter, sugar, and corn syrup. Heat and stir over medium heat until sugar is dissolved. Transfer to a large bowl. Stir in vanilla; let cool 5 minutes.
3. Add beaten egg to butter mixture, mixing well. Beat in flour mixture until well combined. Divide dough into three portions. Cover; chill at least 2 hours or overnight. Let stand at room temperature 30 minutes to soften slightly before rolling. Repeat with a second batch of dough.

SHAPE AND BAKE THE DOUGH

Preheat oven to 375°F. Transfer one portion of dough to work surface; roll between parchment to ⅛- to ¼-inch thickness. Arrange some pattern pieces, page 156 on dough, leaving at least 1 inch between pieces. Cut around the pattern pieces. Remove scraps; set aside for rerolling. Using a small knife or a ½-inch square aspic cutter, cut out window panes on front and sides, keeping muntins intact. Using a knife or a 1-inch teardrop-shape cutter, cut out attic windows. Knead 2 tsp. all-purpose flour into ¼ cup of scraps; roll into thin ropes to form door and window frames.

Transfer cut pieces of dough on parchment to baking sheet. Bake 11 to 13 minutes or until edges are light brown and centers are firm. (If cookie cutouts spread during baking, carefully trim edges while hot.) Using a wooden skewer, reshape window openings. Cool on cookie sheet 1 minute. Transfer on parchment to wire racks; cool completely. Repeat rolling, cutting, and baking until all pattern pieces are made. (They should be completely dry and crisp. If pieces soften, heat in a 325°F oven 10 minutes to recrisp.)

Chai Spice Blend In a bowl combine 1 Tbsp. ground ginger; 1 tsp. each ground cinnamon, ground cardamom, and ground allspice; and ½ tsp. each ground cloves and black pepper. Makes about 2 Tbsp.

DECORATIONS

1 recipe Royal Icing (page 77)
Red and blue gel or paste food coloring
Red rolled fruit leather
Small fresh thyme sprigs tied with gold
    bakers twine
Red licorice ropes
12 oz. vanilla-flavor candy coating
Crème-filled pirouette cookies
Fresh rosemary sprigs
Brown and white jelly beans
Coarse white sugar

TO DECORATE

Make Royal Icing; it will be used to attach all pieces and to decorate the cottage. Tint ¼ cup Royal Icing with red food coloring and ¼ cup with blue food coloring, then transfer to separate pastry bags fitted with small open tips. Transfer the remaining white icing to a large pastry bag fitted with a large open tip. Cover the work surface with parchment paper. Spread white Royal Icing onto the awning. Let dry. Place cottage front wrong side up; attach fruit leather as curtains. Let dry 15 minutes. Turn front face up. Attach tied thyme sprigs above windows. Attach decorated awning; pipe details as desired. Twist licorice rope into a wreath shape; tie with ribbon. Secure wreath above door. Let dry 1 hour.

ASSEMBLE WALLS

Build the cottage on a large flat tray or cutting board. Using heavy objects (such as tumblers or vegetable cans) to hold pieces in place, prop up the front wall. Pipe icing onto the edges of front wall and one side wall. Attach the side wall, using tumblers or cans to hold in place. Repeat with all walls. Let dry 2 hours.

DECORATE ROOF

In a medium microwave-safe dish heat candy coating 1 minute. Stir; heat 1 minute more or until melted and smooth. Stir once more. Spread coating onto parchment paper in a thin layer to form an 11×14-inch rectangle. Let set until firm, about 1 hour. Spread a thin layer of Royal Icing over a roof piece. Break candy coating into irregular bits; arrange bits in rows on wet icing, working from the bottom up across the width until covered. Repeat for opposite side of roof.

ASSEMBLE ROOF

Pipe icing along the top edges of one side of the cottage. Spread a ½-inch-thick layer of icing in a 1-inch-wide band on the

back side of a roof piece along the side and bottom edges where it will attach to the cottage. Set roof piece on wall edges; press gently to adhere to icing. Standard vegetable cans are the correct height to support roof while it dries. Repeat with opposite roof. Pipe a line of icing along center of roof where the two halves meet; cover with Pirouette cookies trimmed to fit. Let dry at least 2 hours.

BUILD PLANTER

To decorate planter fronts, spread Royal Icing onto two short and two long sections; use a fork or toothpick to create texture in icing. Pipe a generous strip of icing onto remaining planter pieces. Place rosemary sprigs on icing strips. Top rosemary with decorated pieces, textured sides up. Let dry 30 minutes. For sparkly lights, pipe blue Royal Icing onto tips of rosemary sprigs. Attach planters to front and sides of cottage.

FINISHING TOUCHES

Use Royal Icing to draw a path to the front door; attach jelly beans. Sprinkle the tray with coarse white sugar. If desired, decorate with mini peppermint candy trees and dust roof with powdered sugar.

ROYAL ICING

In a large bowl stir together 4 cups powdered sugar, 3 Tbsp. meringue powder, and ½ tsp. cream of tartar. Add ½ cup warm water and 1 tsp. vanilla. Beat with an electric mixer on low until combined, then on high 7 to 10 minutes or until very stiff. When not using, cover bowl with a damp paper towel; cover tightly with plastic wrap. (Icing dries out quickly when exposed to air.) Chill up to 48 hours. Stir before using. Makes 3 cups.

Pillows Aplenty

Holiday pillows add instant cheer to any room.

FELT FOREST

A little red bird perches on a birch limb on this cozy ready-made wool pillow. Use the patterns on page 155 to cut out the ivory felt trees, then add horizontal straight stitches to give each tree distinctive striations. Cut out the bird from red felt; stitch to the pillow.

SUBTLE BEAUTY

Throw pillows in wintry colors and soft-texture fabrics make it fun to adapt a home for the holiday season. The flowers on this dimensional pillow bloom three subtle shades of wool felt.

WHAT YOU NEED

Die-cutting tool and flower dies or scissors
Wood felt in white, natural, and oatmeal
Ivory sewing thread
Sewing needle
¾-inch cover button kit
15-inch-square ivory pillow sham
15-inch-square pillow form

WHAT YOU DO

1. Cut the flowers using a die-cutting tool. Or, using the patterns on page 156, trace one small, one medium, and one large poinsettia bract cluster and one small, one medium, and one large chrysanthemum petal cluster onto white paper; cut out. For each poinsettia, cut one small bract cluster from white wool felt, one medium bract cluster from natural felt, and one large bract cluster from oatmeal felt (the pillow shown has three poinsettias). For each chrysanthemum, cut one small, one medium, and one large petal cluster from oatmeal felt (the pillow shown has two chrysanthemums). For looped flowers, cut one 3½×36-inch, one 2½×36-inch, and one 1½×36-inch strip from white felt.

2. For each poinsettia, refer to the patterns for placement. Pin and sew a fold in each bract in each cluster. With folded sides down, stack the three clusters, largest to smallest. Sew layers together with small stitches in the center.

3. For each chrysanthemum, stack three petal clusters, largest to smallest. Sew layers together with small stitches in center.

4. Arrange poinsettias and chrysanthemums on pillow cover, allowing space for looped flowers (pillow shown has five looped flowers). Sew poinsettias and chrysanthemums to the pillow cover with small stitches in flower centers.

5. Following manufacturer's directions, cover buttons with oatmeal felt. Sew a button to pillow cover where the center of a looped flower is desired. Fold each felt strip in half lengthwise and sew the cut edges together, forming a tube. Cutting to

but not through the stitching, cut slits ¼ inch apart along the folded edge.

6. Starting with an end of smallest tube, tuck sewn edge under button and wind tube in a circle around base of button. Using small stitches, hand-stitch sewn edge to pillow cover. Circle button with a second row of the tube, enlarging circle so second row of looped petals extends beyond first. Continue hand-stitching tube in place.

7. Leaving the thread connected, cut off remaining tube (save for next flower).

Switch to the medium tube. Stitch the end of the new tube near the end of the smaller tube. Continue to circle the button and stitch the tube to the pillow. Cut off the remaining medium tube and use the largest tube to make the final circle of looped petals.

8. Stuff pillow insert into pillow sham.

PLAID PUNCH

Heighten holiday decor by stitching up woodsy throw pillows. Felt silhouettes of Santa's nimble navigators fused onto readymade plaid pillow covers add a hint of wilderness to a cozy sofa or inviting entry bench. For the design, lay fusible web, paper side up, over reindeer pattern on page 156. Use a pencil to trace pattern. Cut out fusible-web shape roughly ¼ inch outside traced lines. Following manufacturer's instructions, press fusible-web shape onto felt; let cool. Cut out shape on drawn lines. Peel off paper backing. Center and fuse reindeer appliqué on one plaid flannel square. Insert pillow form into cover.

HOLIDAY SPEAK

Accent a sofa or chair with this festive pillow decked for the season. Amid white felt lettering on a creamy linen pillowcase, a green felt wreath punched with whimsical lime green pom-poms makes a clever holiday statement.

WHAT YOU NEED
Paper, pencil scissors
Fusible web
Felt in white and sage green
11½×16½-inch piece of cream linen fabric for pillow top
Two 11½-inch squares of cream linen fabric for pillow back
Pinking shears
Cream sewing thread
Hot-glue gun and glue sticks
½-inch-diameter lime green pom-poms
11×16-inch pillow form

WHAT YOU DO
1. Use the patterns from page 155 to trace the leaf onto white paper; cut out. Trace letter patterns onto the paper side of fusible web, leaving ½ inch between each letter. Cut out each fusible-web letter roughly ¼ inch beyond traced lines. Following manufacturer's instructions, press fusible-web letters onto white felt; cut out letters on drawn lines.
2. Turn under ½ inch of one edge of each 11½-inch cream square; press. Turn under ½ inch again on same edges then stitch in place using cream thread.
3. Overlap hemmed edges of pillow back pieces 4½ inches to make an 11½×16½-inch rectangle. Baste overlapped edges to make pillow back.
4. Layer pillow front and pillow back with right sides together. Stitch around all edges. Turn right side out.
5. Arrange felt letters to butt up to each narrow edge on pillow front, leaving space for the O. Arrange overlapping sage green felt leaves in a circle for the O. Hot-glue leaves in place. Hot-glue pom-poms on leaves. Peel off paper backings on felt letters; press. Insert pillow form through opening in back.

CELEBRATORY SETTING

Break away from holiday hues with a fresh palette of pinks and blues. The color combination gets nudged into pure class with the addition of silver and black.

Ring It In

Bring glamour and glitz to your New Year's celebration with sparkly accents and luscious hues. These tabletop accents start the year stylishly fresh.

FLOWERS 'N' FLICKER

For a stunning centerpiece, set a pillar candle in a glass vessel. Partially fill the bowl with water and cut flowers to fit around the candle. Arrange taller stems to one side of the arrangement for drama.

CLASSY PLACE CARDS

Set the table with a pretty placecard directing guests to their seats. Fold a 3×6-inch piece of cardstock in half, narrow ends together. Trim the front of the place card with blue and pink ribbon and silver chenille stem pieces, hot-glued in place.

STRIPED CRACKERS

Wrapping paper tubes, cut into 6-inch lengths, become vessels to hold wrapped chocolates or other small candies. Cut glittery silver wrapping paper to go around each tube, allowing 3 extra inches beyond each end; tape in place. Cut paper strips to trim the cracker; hot-glue around the wrapped tube. Pinch the wrapping paper at one end of the tube; secure with ribbon. Fill the cracker through the open end, then tie closed with a second piece of ribbon.

PARTY POLKA DOTS

Make color-coordinated confetti to brighten the dining table. Punch various-size circles from glittery papers to place color side up on the table.

PICTURE-PERFECT TRAY

Paper strips, woven together in various widths, make a beautiful insert for a 12-inch-square picture frame turned serving tray. To secure the backing, cut a thin piece of plywood the same size as the frame back; paint to match frame and let dry. Drill holes through the backing board and into the frame. Use small wood screws to attach the plywood to the frame bottom.

CANDLE CUBBIES

Recycle peanut cans into candleholders with just a couple of shimmery embellishments. Cut two glittery paper strips to wrap the can; hot-glue in place. Cover the seam with chenille stem. Add a cluster of three small plastic ornaments, along with two chenille stem loops.

Flip Your Lid

FRIENDLY FACE

Craft a cheery snowman topped with a laundry detergent lid for a hat. Wrap a plastic-foam ball with white yarn, tacking in place with low-temp glue. Create eyes and a mouth with map pins and an upholstery tack for a nose. Spray-paint the lid black; let dry. Cut a black felt circle slightly larger than the lid. Hot-glue the lid to the brim and the hat to the top of the snowman head. Trim the hat with chenille stem and a pom-pom. Tie a knot in a narrow ribbon and glue to the base of the ornament.

ORNAMENT STAND

Display special ornaments on elegant silvery stands that show off ridges and details. Use spray paint to dress up large lids, such as those from detergent and juice bottles; allow to dry. Use the natural cradles to hold ornaments upright.

GOODIE CUP

A large, deep lid trimmed with ribbon and cord becomes a showy treat cup. For a different color, spray-paint the cup and let it dry before gluing on the trims.

RECYCLE STYLE

Holiday greeting cards get a second go-'round as darling ornaments. For backing, use the ends of frozen juice containers and hot-glue cut-out designs from cards onto one side. Hot-glue metallic chenille stem around the edge of the lid; add a ribbon bow to the bottom and a hanging loop to the top.

ONE COOL COASTER

Plastic or metal, large jar lids make clever coasters. Spray-paint the lid light blue; let dry. Trace around the lid on felt and trim inside the circle with pinking shears. Hot-glue the felt to the inside of the lid and a piece of narrow ribbon around the edge. A snowflake trim hides the ribbon seam.

ONE DOUGH, FIVE WAYS
Recipes on page 109

food

Whether it's a celebratory brunch, a formal feast, a casual meal for a cozy night in—or a trayful of gorgeous homemade cookies—it's sharing time around the table with loved ones that makes the holidays special.

CHOCOLATE-PECAN COFFEE CAKE
Recipe on page 94

Best Holiday Brunch

Put on this elegant brunch early in the day and you can relax the rest of it. There's something on the menu for everyone—sweet and savory, decadent and indulgent, and light and healthful.

CRANBERRY-
RASPBERRY
SPRITZ

CRANBERRY-RASPBERRY SPRITZ

Sparkle and flavor pack these glass-clinking drinks. They're designed to cheer the holidays.

PREP 20 minutes
CHILL 2 hours

WHAT YOU NEED

3   cups sugar
2   cups water
1   12-oz. pkg. cranberries
1   12-oz. pkg. frozen unsweetened raspberries
   Champagne, carbonated water, or lemon-lime carbonated beverage, chilled
   Fresh raspberries and/or cranberries for garnish (optional)

WHAT YOU DO

1. In a medium saucepan combine sugar, water, cranberries, and raspberries. Bring to boiling; reduce heat to medium. Simmer, uncovered, about 5 minutes until all the cranberries have popped. Remove from heat and allow to cool to room temperature. Pass through a fine-mesh sieve, pressing lightly on the fruit with the back of a large spoon. Do not press too hard or syrup may become cloudy. Transfer syrup to a pitcher or bottle; cover and refrigerate until ready to use, at least 2 hours. Syrup may be refrigerated up to 2 weeks.

2. When ready to serve, place about 1 Tbsp. of the chilled syrup in a champagne flute or wine glass and top with chilled champagne, carbonated water, or carbonated lemon-lime beverage. Stir gently and garnish with fresh raspberries and/or cranberries threaded on a skewer, if desired. Makes about 5 cups syrup. Makes 80 servings.

BABY POTATOES ROASTED IN SALT

BABY POTATOES ROASTED IN SALT

The salt crust is intended only to create a crisp exterior on the potatoes. It will be very hard—eat only the potatoes!

PREP 25 minutes
COOL 5 minutes
ROAST 45 minutes

WHAT YOU NEED

¼   cup olive oil
4   cloves garlic, minced
3   Tbsp. snipped fresh rosemary
30 small new potatoes and/or fingerling potatoes (about 3 lb.)
1½ lb. kosher salt (3 cups)
¼   cup all-purpose flour
½   cup water
   Freshly ground black pepper

WHAT YOU DO

1. Preheat oven to 425°F. In a small bowl combine 2 Tbsp. of the oil and the garlic. Brush mixture on the bottom and sides of a 2½- to 3-qt. gratin dish or shallow baking dish. Sprinkle rosemary in dish. Place potatoes in a single layer on top of rosemary.

2. In a large bow combine salt and flour. Gradually stir in water until combined. Spoon salt mixture evenly over potatoes, pressing firmly.

3. Roast 45 to 50 minutes or until potatoes are tender. Cool on a wire rack 5 minutes. Using a thin metal spatula, loosen the salt crust from the side of the dish. Carefully invert potatoes and salt crust onto a large serving platter. Drizzle potatoes with the remaining 2 Tbsp. oil and sprinkle with pepper. Makes 15 servings.

ARUGULA, CORN, AND
TOMATO SALAD WITH
RICOTTA SALATA

ARUGULA, CORN, AND TOMATO SALAD WITH RICOTTA SALATA

Ricotta salata—a fresh cheese with a briny taste and a grainy yet sliceable texture—is made with whey rather than milk.

START TO FINISH 25 minutes

WHAT YOU NEED

6   cups fresh arugula
1½   cups fresh basil leaves, torn
1½   cups fresh or frozen whole kernel corn, thawed
1   cup halved cherry tomatoes
3   Tbsp. olive oil
2   Tbsp. lemon juice
¼   tsp. salt
⅛   tsp. ground black pepper
2½   oz. ricotta salata

WHAT YOU DO

1. In a large bowl combine arugula, basil, corn, and tomatoes.
2. For dressing, in a small bowl whisk together oil, lemon juice, salt, and pepper. Drizzle dressing over arugula mixture; toss to coat. Transfer to a serving platter. Crumble cheese over salad. Makes 8 servings.

CHOCOLATE-PECAN COFFEE CAKE

The filling for this decadent treat is a gooey combination of brown sugar, butter, cinnamon, coconut, pecans, and semisweet chocolate.

PREP 30 minutes
BAKE 55 minutes
COOL 20 minutes

WHAT YOU NEED

½   cup butter, softened
1   cup granulated sugar
2   tsp. baking powder
½   tsp. baking soda
¼   tsp. salt
2   eggs
1   tsp. vanilla
2¼   cups all-purpose flour
1   8-oz. carton dairy sour cream
1   recipe Coconut-Pecan Topping

WHAT YOU DO

1. Preheat oven to 325°F. Grease and flour a 10-inch fluted tube pan; set aside. In a large mixing bowl beat butter with a mixer on medium to high for 30 seconds. Add the sugar, baking powder, baking soda, and salt. Beat until well combined, scraping sides of bowl occasionally. Add eggs one at a time, beating well after each addition. Beat in vanilla. Alternately add flour and sour cream to butter mixture, beating on low after each addition just until combined.
2. Sprinkle half of the Coconut-Pecan Topping in the prepared pan. Spoon half of the cake batter in mounds over the coconut mixture. Carefully spread to an even layer. Sprinkle with remaining Coconut-Pecan Topping. Spoon on remaining cake batter and spread to an even layer.
3. Bake 55 to 65 minutes or until a long wooden skewer inserted near the center comes out clean. Cool on a wire rack 20 minutes. Turn out of pan. Serve warm. Makes 12 servings.

Coconut-Pecan Topping In a medium bowl stir together 1 cup all-purpose flour, 1 cup packed brown sugar, and 1 tsp. ground cinnamon. Using a pastry blender, cut in ½ cup cold butter until mixture resembles coarse crumbs. Stir in ¾ cup semisweet chocolate pieces, ½ cup flaked coconut, and ½ cup chopped pecans.

Cinnamon-Nut Coffee Cake Prepare as directed, except omit chocolate pieces and coconut in the Coconut-Pecan Topping and increase pecans to 1 cup.

CHOCOLATE-PECAN
COFFEE CAKE

AMARETTO
BRIOCHE BAKE

AMARETTO BRIOCHE BAKE

Brioche—a rich bread made with butter and eggs—gives this breakfast bake luxurious taste and texture.

PREP 20 minutes
CHILL 4 hours
BAKE 40 minutes
STAND 15 minutes

WHAT YOU NEED

- 1 cup packed brown sugar
- ⅓ cup butter
- ¼ cup amaretto
- 2 Tbsp. light-color corn syrup
- 1 12-oz. loaf brioche or other sweet bread, cut into 8 slices
- 4 eggs, lightly beaten
- 2 cups half-and-half, light cream, or milk
- 1½ tsp. vanilla
- ½ tsp. salt
- ¼ tsp. ground nutmeg or cardamom
  Fresh blackberries (optional)
  Powdered sugar (optional)

WHAT YOU DO

1. Preheat oven to 350°F. Lightly grease a 3-qt. rectangular baking dish; set aside. In a medium saucepan combine brown sugar, butter, amaretto, and corn syrup. Cook and stir until boiling. Boil, uncovered, 1 minute. Pour into the prepared baking dish. Arrange bread slices on brown sugar mixture.

2. In a medium bowl combine eggs, half-and-half, vanilla, salt, and nutmeg. Pour evenly over bread slices. Using the back of a wide spatula, lightly press bread down to soak with egg mixture. Cover and chill 4 to 24 hours.

3. Bake, uncovered, for 40 to 45 minutes or until a knife inserted near the center comes out clean and the top is lightly browned. Let stand 15 minutes before serving.

4. If desired, top with blackberries and sprinkle with powdered sugar. Makes 8 servings.

MACERATED GRAPEFRUIT WITH PISTACHIOS AND POMEGRANATE

MACERATED GRAPEFRUIT WITH PISTACHIOS AND POMEGRANATE

Macerating is to simply soak in liquid. In this case, slices of grapefruit bathe in a combination of grapefruit juice, honey, and coriander. As the mixture sits, even more liquid is extracted from the fruit, creating a delicious syrup to drizzle over the grapefruit slices.

PREP 25 minutes
CHILL 1 hour

WHAT YOU NEED

- ½ cup unsweetened pink grapefruit juice
- ¼ cup honey
- ½ tsp. ground coriander
- 4 large pink, red, and/or white grapefruits
- ¼ cup coarsely chopped pistachio nuts, macadamia nuts, hazelnuts (filberts), pecans, cashews, or pine nuts
- ¼ cup pomegranate seeds, toasted flaked coconut, finely chopped maraschino cherries, plain Greek yogurt, or 1 to 2 tsp. orange, lemon, or lime zest

WHAT YOU DO

1. In a small bowl combine grapefruit juice, honey, and coriander. Mix well and set aside.

2. With a sharp knife, remove skin and white membrane from grapefruits. Slice grapefruits crosswise into ¼-inch-thick rounds. Transfer slices to a large wide-mouth jar; add the grapefruit juice mixture. Cover and chill at least 1 hour or up to 5 days.

3. To serve, arrange grapefruit slices on a serving platter; pour liquid over slices. Top with pistachio nuts, pomegranate seeds and dollops of yogurt. Serve immediately. Makes 8 servings.

BREAKFAST HAM AND EGG CUPS

BACON-AND-CHEESE DEVILED EGGS

Everybody loves deviled eggs—adding smoky bacon and sharp cheddar cheese makes them even better. They can be made and chilled in the refrigerator a day ahead—just be sure to garnish right before serving.

START TO FINISH 25 minutes

WHAT YOU NEED

12 hard-cooked eggs
½ cup mayonnaise or salad dressing
1 Tbsp. honey mustard
¼ tsp. salt
¼ tsp. ground black pepper
4 slices bacon, crisp-cooked, drained, and crumbled
2 Tbsp. shredded sharp cheddar cheese
   Bacon, crisp-cooked, drained, and crumbled (optional)
   Chopped green onions (optional)
   Shredded sharp cheddar (optional)

WHAT YOU DO

1. Halve hard-cooked eggs lengthwise and remove yolks. Set whites aside. Place yolks in a small bowl; mash with a fork. Stir in mayonnaise, honey mustard, salt, and pepper. Fold in the 4 slices crumbled bacon and the 2 Tbsp. cheese.
2. Stuff egg white halves with yolk mixture. Chill until ready to serve.
3. Right before serving, top eggs with additional crumbled bacon, green onions and cheddar cheese, if desired. Makes 12 servings.

BREAKFAST HAM AND EGG CUPS

When baked, thin slices of ham create crispy cups to hold eggs, cheese, pesto, and tomatoes in these low-carb breakfast bites.

PREP 20 minutes
BAKE 18 minutes
STAND 3 minutes

WHAT YOU NEED

   Nonstick cooking spray
8 thin slices deli-style cooked ham
¼ cup shredded Italian cheese blend or mozzarella cheese (1 oz.)
8 eggs
   Ground black pepper
8 tsp. basil pesto (optional)
8 cherry tomatoes or grape tomatoes, halved

WHAT YOU DO

1. Preheat oven to 350°F. Coat eight 2½-inch muffin cups with cooking spray. Gently press a ham slice onto the bottom and up the sides of each prepared muffin cup, carefully ruffling the edges of ham. Divide cheese among the ham-lined muffin cups.
2. Break an egg into a measuring cup and slip egg into a muffin cup. Repeat with the remaining eggs. Sprinkle with pepper. If desired, spoon 1 tsp. of the pesto onto each egg. Top with tomato halves.
3. Bake 18 to 20 minutes or until whites are completely set and yolks are thickened. Let stand in muffin cups 3 to 5 minutes before serving. Carefully remove egg cups from muffin cups. Makes 8 servings.

BACON-AND-CHEESE
DEVILED EGGS

An Easy-Cooking Holiday Feast

Follow this step-by-step plan to make dinner in about 3 hours. Then serve an herb-crusted roast, cheddar biscuits, creamy scalloped potatoes, and Brussels sprouts—all in stress-free style.

Step 1 Start with Scalloped Russet and Sweet Potatoes. Try slicing the potatoes with a mandoline. The inexpensive models—about $10 to $15—work just fine.

Step 2 Assemble Herb-and-Garlic-Crusted Pork Roast, then set aside. Letting it stand up to 1 hour before cooking helps the crumbs adhere.

Step 3 Putting together the Plum Compote is a 10-minute task. It simmers on a back burner while you fix the Brussels sprouts.

Step 4 While preheating the oven for the roast, halve and trim the Brussels sprouts, then tuck them away in the refrigerator. They'll cook while the biscuits bake.

Step 5 Once the roast and potatoes are in the oven, get to work on the Double-Cheddar Holiday Biscuits. Mix, roll, and cut out the dough. Arrange on a baking sheet, then set aside in the refrigerator.

HERB-AND-GARLIC-CRUSTED PORK ROAST

The pork roast can sit in the brine up to 2 days before you plan to cook it. Soaking the meat in a sugar-and-salt solution enhances its flavor and makes this lean roast super juicy.

PREP 25 minutes
MARINATE overnight
ROAST 1 hour
STAND 15 minutes

WHAT YOU NEED

- ½   cup kosher salt
- ¼   cup brown sugar
- 8   cups cold water
- 1   center cut, boneless pork loin, approximately 3 to 3½ lb.*
- 3   Tbsp. peanut or vegetable oil
- 4   slices Black Forest bacon or other thick-sliced bacon, cut in 1-inch pieces (uncooked)
- 1   Tbsp. apricot preserves
- 2   tsp. finely chopped fresh garlic
- 1   Tbsp. chopped fresh rosemary
- 1½ cups fresh bread crumbs**
- 3   Tbsp. chopped fresh parsley
- ½   tsp. kosher salt
     Freshly ground black pepper
- 3   Tbsp. butter, melted

WHAT YOU DO

1. For brine, in an extra-large bowl dissolve salt and sugar in 8 cups cold water. Transfer pork to brine, making sure to submerge it fully. Cover and refrigerate overnight, or up to 2 days.

2. Remove loin from brine and blot dry with paper towels. In a nonstick skillet heat oil, then brown roast on all sides, about 10 minutes. Set aside 5 to 30 minutes to cool slightly.

3. In a food processor puree uncooked bacon to a smooth paste. (This amount of bacon is necessary for blades to process.) Transfer half the bacon to a bowl. Stir in apricot preserves, chopped garlic, and 2 tsp. of the chopped rosemary.

4. Position oven rack in lowest position. Preheat oven to 425°F. Place cooled pork loin on waxed paper. Spread with bacon mixture. In a separate bowl combine the bread crumbs, parsley, remaining rosemary, ½ tsp. kosher salt, a few grinds of black pepper, and the melted butter. Toss well to mix. Press an even layer of the crumb mixture on the roast (except the ends), applying enough pressure for the crumbs to adhere to the bacon layer.

PLUM COMPOTE

HERB-AND-GARLIC-CRUSTED PORK ROAST

5. Transfer roast to a wire rack in a foil-lined baking pan or roasting pan. Roast 15 minutes. Reduce oven temperature to 350°F. Roast 45 minutes more or until an instant-read thermometer registers 145°F. (If crust begins to brown too deeply, tent roast with foil.) Remove roast from oven, tent with foil, and allow to rest 15 minutes in a warm place. Temperature of roast will rise approximately 10°F as it stands. Makes servings.

* If you do not use a natural pork roast, skip the brining step.

** If you don't let the crumbs stale overnight, spread them in a 15×10×1-inch baking pan and bake, uncovered, in a 300°F oven 10 minutes or until dry, stirring once or twice. Crumbs will continue to dry as they cool.

Menu Planning Tips

- Increase oven to 425°F. When it reaches 425°F, bake biscuits while roast and potatoes rest.
- Reserve any unused seasoned bread crumbs and store in the freezer.
- Serve with plum pudding compote and a dish of Dijon-style mustard on the side.
- Slices of cold roast pork are excellent for sandwiches or midnight snacks, especially with a bit of the compote.
- Use some of the remaining bacon puree to spread on baguette slices and toast until golden. Serve with cheese and plum pudding compote.

PLUM COMPOTE

Pork and fruit pair naturally. This make-ahead fruit sauce is a lovely combination of dried plums, apricots, apples, and cherries cooked in port wine with sugar, salt, and bay leaf.

PREP 10 minutes
COOK 50 minutes

WHAT YOU NEED

- 1   cup pitted prunes
- 1   cup dried apricots
- ¾   cup dried apple slices, halved
- ½   cup dried cherries
- 3   fresh bay leaves (or 1 dried bay leaf)
- ¼   cup granulated sugar
- ¼   tsp. kosher salt
- 3   cups port wine or cranberry juice

WHAT YOU DO

1. Combine all ingredients in a nonreactive medium-size saucepan. Bring to simmering. Cover partially, and simmer very slowly 40 minutes. Uncover and simmer 10 minutes longer or until the fruit is tender and the port is slightly reduced and thickened. Remove and discard bay leaves. Makes 12 servings.

Variation If desired, chop dried fruit prior to cooking to make a spreadable compote.

Storage Cover tightly and store, refrigerated, up to 5 days.

DOUBLE-CHEDDAR HOLIDAY BISCUITS

Two types of cheese—extra-sharp white cheddar and sharp orange cheddar—flavor these buttermilk biscuits.

PREP 20 minutes
BAKE 16 minutes
COOL 5 minutes

WHAT YOU NEED

5   cups unbleached all-purpose flour, sifted before measuring
1   Tbsp. plus 1 tsp. baking powder*
2½   tsp. kosher salt
1   tsp. granulated sugar
⅛   tsp. cayenne pepper
4   oz. shredded extra-sharp white cheddar cheese, room temperature (about 1 cup)
4   oz. shredded sharp orange cheddar cheese, room temperature (about 1 cup)
6   Tbsp. cold unsalted butter, cut in ½-inch pieces
2   cups heavy cream
¼   cup buttermilk

WHAT YOU DO

1. Position a rack in the center of the oven. Preheat oven to 425°F. Line a baking sheet with foil. In a large mixing bowl whisk together the flour, baking powder, salt, sugar, and cayenne. Add shredded cheeses, then work in well with your fingers. Add the cold butter. Quickly rub butter into flour mixture with fingers until mixture resembles the texture of oatmeal with some large marble-size pieces.

2. Stir in the heavy cream; add buttermilk and stir just until absorbed. Dough will be chunky and dry at this point. Turn out dough onto a lightly floured board. Using your hand, press and knead into a cohesive dough. (This will take a bit of pressure. Fear not. This is a sturdy, forgiving dough, not a fluffy light one.)

3. Roll dough to ½-inch thickness. With a fork dipped in flour, prick evenly spaced holes all over the dough. Stamp out 2½-inch rounds and place about ½ inch apart on lined baking sheet. Gather dough pieces, reroll, cut out, and place on baking sheet. (At this stage the biscuits can be lightly covered and refrigerated 1 hour before baking.)

4. Bake biscuits 16 to 18 minutes, until well browned, rotating pan if needed to ensure even browning. Cool slightly before serving. (To reheat biscuits, warm at 350°F 3 to 5 minutes.) Makes 26 servings.

***Homemade Baking Powder** In a small bowl combine ¼ cup cream of tartar and 2 Tbsp. baking soda. Sift together three times. Transfer to a clean tight-sealing jar. Store at room temperature, away from sunlight, up to 6 weeks.

Storage Tip Store baked biscuits at room temperature up to 3 days or freeze up to 1 month. Remove biscuits from freezer and thaw at room temperature. Reheat 3 to 5 minutes at 350°F.

DOUBLE-CHEDDAR HOLIDAY BISCUITS

CARAMELIZED BRUSSELS SPROUTS WITH LEMON

CARAMELIZED BRUSSELS SPROUTS WITH LEMON

Cooking the Brussels sprouts cut sides down in the pan creates a yummy golden brown crust, so be sure not to stir them until they're tender.

PREP 15 minutes
COOK 6 minutes

WHAT YOU NEED

¼   cup extra-virgin olive oil
4   cups Brussels sprouts, rinsed, trimmed, and halved lengthwise
     Salt and freshly ground black pepper
2   Tbsp. water
     Juice of half a lemon, about 1 Tbsp.

WHAT YOU DO

1. In a 12-inch nonstick skillet heat 3 Tbsp. of the oil over medium heat. Arrange sprouts in a single layer, cut sides down. Drizzle with remaining olive oil and sprinkle generously with salt and a grind or two of black pepper. Cover and cook 3 minutes. Remove lid and sprinkle sprouts with water. Cover and cook for 2 minutes more. Sprouts should just be beginning to caramelize and, when pierced with a fork, slightly tender.

2. Remove cover and increase heat slightly. When cut sides are well-caramelized, toss Brussels sprouts in pan, drizzle with lemon juice, and sprinkle with more salt and pepper to taste. Makes 6 servings.

SCALLOPED RUSSET AND SWEET POTATOES

A single sweet potato adds color and a touch of sweetness to this creamy potato gratin. Grate the whole nutmeg on a microplane grater. You will be amazed at the difference freshly grated nutmeg makes!

PREP 50 minutes
BAKE 55 minutes
STAND 10 minutes

WHAT YOU NEED

1   clove garlic
1   Tbsp. butter, softened
1   large onion, peeled
2   Tbsp. olive oil
     Kosher salt and freshly ground black pepper to taste
½   tsp. snipped fresh thyme
2   cups milk
½   cup heavy cream
3   Tbsp. butter
3   Tbsp. all-purpose flour
5   medium russet potatoes
1   medium sweet potato
     Whole nutmeg

WHAT YOU DO

1. Preheat oven to 350°F. Aggressively rub the inside of a 2½- to 3-qt. gratin dish or 3-qt. rectangular baking dish with garlic clove. Generously butter the dish; set aside.

2. Cut onion in half. Using a mandoline or knife, slice the onion halves very thinly, approximately ¹⁄₁₆ inch thick (⅛ inch with a knife). Warm the olive oil in a large skillet. Cook onion gently, until tender and translucent, seasoning well with salt and pepper and stirring in thyme leaves at the end.

3. In a medium saucepan heat milk and cream just until simmering. In a large saucepan melt 3 Tbsp. butter over medium heat. Whisk in the flour. Remove from heat and gradually whisk in hot milk and cream. Return to heat and bring to boiling, whisking or stirring constantly. Boil gently 3 to 5 minutes or until thickened and the consistency of buttermilk.

4. Peel russet and sweet potatoes. Very thinly slice potatoes on a mandoline to approximately ¹⁄₁₆-inch thickness or slice thinly with a sharp knife. Layer one-third of the potatoes in baking dish. Season generously with salt and pepper; sprinkle lightly with freshly grated nutmeg. Top with one-third of the onions and some of the sauce. Repeat layering in thirds, finishing with sauce (the cream may not totally cover top).

5. Bake uncovered 45 minutes. Increase oven temperature to 425°F. Bake 10 to 15 minutes more or until bubbly, golden crusty brown, and potatoes are tender when pierced with a wooden pick. Remove from oven. Let stand 10 minutes before serving. Makes 8 servings.

Make Ahead Slice the potatoes up to 1 day ahead and keep them in the refrigerator in a bowl with enough water to cover. Drain well and pat dry with paper towels before using.

SCALLOPED RUSSET AND SWEET POTATOES

Casual Comfort

Skip the fuss this season and create a hearty, soul-soothing supper—whether it's for a special holiday dinner or a cozy night in. This simple, affordable meal can bend to fit your schedule. You can easily prepare it all in one day or spread out bits of prep over a few days.

Make-Ahead Tips A few days before, cut up and salt the meat. It can rest in the fridge up to 2 days, and the flavor improves as the seasoning has time to permeate the meat. You can also make the entire stew up to 2 days before. It thickens and the flavors mature and ripen. Just skim off any fat from the top and warm through before serving.

The day before, make the puddings and have the syrup for the compote prepped and ready to toss with the fruit just before serving.

An hour before serving, if desired, prepare the broccoli (it can be eaten warm or at room temperature) while you make the spoon bread.

CORNMEAL SPOON BREAD

If you can't find fine-ground white cornmeal, regular cornmeal is fine.

PREP 35 minutes
COOL 15 minutes
BAKE 30 minutes

WHAT YOU NEED

5 Tbsp. unsalted butter, softened
4 cups milk
1 cup fine-ground white cornmeal
1 tsp. kosher salt
1 tsp. sugar
4 eggs, separated
⅛ tsp. cream of tartar

WHAT YOU DO

1. Preheat oven to 400°F. Butter a 1½-qt. soufflé dish with 2 Tbsp. of the butter; set aside.

2. In a large saucepan heat milk just until below boiling. Slowly whisk in cornmeal; bring to boiling. Cook, whisking constantly, over medium heat about 5 minutes or until mixture thickens and begins to pull away from the sides of the saucepan. Remove from heat; transfer to a large mixing bowl. Cool 10 minutes. Whisk in the remaining 3 Tbsp. butter, salt, and sugar. Beat in egg yolks until well blended.

3. In a large clean mixing bowl beat egg whites and cream of tartar with a large clean whisk until they form soft glossy mounds. Stir one-third of the beaten egg whites into cornmeal mixture to lighten. Gently fold in remaining egg whites. Gently turn into prepared soufflé dish (batter will nearly fill the dish). Bake 30 minutes or until puffed and golden brown. Cool 5 minutes before serving. Makes 8 servings.

BUTTERMILK PUDDING WITH POMEGRANATE COMPOTE

When the gelatin is softened in the milk, it will look like a wad of gum—but you haven't done anything wrong. This helps the gelatin dissolve into the hot cream.

PREP 25 minutes
COOK 10 minutes
CHILL 2 hours

WHAT YOU NEED

¼ cup cold milk or water
2 envelopes unflavored gelatin
2 cups heavy cream
1 cup sugar
½ cup crème fraîche
2 cups buttermilk
¼ cup freshly squeezed lemon juice
¾ tsp. vanilla
½ tsp. kosher salt
4 tsp. lemon zest
Pomegranate Compote

WHAT YOU DO

1. In a small bowl combine milk and the gelatin; set aside.

2. In a saucepan bring heavy cream and sugar to a simmer over medium heat, stirring until sugar is completely dissolved. Immediately remove from heat; add gelatin mixture, stirring until completely dissolved. Cool 5 minutes. Transfer to a mixing bowl. Whisk in crème fraîche until blended. Whisk in buttermilk, lemon juice, vanilla, and salt. Strain. Whisk in lemon zest.

3. Divide pudding among eight 8-oz. ramekins. Cover with plastic wrap and chill until set, 2 to 3 hours. Serve with Pomegranate Compote. Makes 8 servings.

Pomegranate Compote In a small saucepan combine ⅓ cup dry red wine and ⅓ cup sugar. Bring to a simmer, stirring to dissolve sugar. Simmer, uncovered, about 3 minutes or until slightly reduced and syrupy. Remove from heat; cool completely. In a small bowl combine ½ cup fresh pomegranate seeds and ¼ cup navel orange sections, chopped. Sprinkle with ⅛ tsp. salt. Pour syrup over pomegranate mixture. Stir 2 teaspoons lemon juice into mixture. Spoon over Buttermilk Pudding.

CORNMEAL SPOON BREAD

BUTTERMILK PUDDING WITH POMEGRANATE COMPOTE

ROASTED BROCCOLI AND OLIVES

Try a few varieties of olives, such as green olives and black niçoise. Find several options at an antipasti or olive bar at your supermarkets and deli counters.

PREP 15 minutes
ROAST 20 minutes

WHAT YOU NEED

6   cloves garlic, peeled and gently crushed
1   tsp. kosher salt, divided
2¼ to 2½ lb. broccoli, washed, drained, and patted dry
¼   cup extra-virgin olive oil, plus more for drizzling
½   cup mixed unpitted olives
    Flaked sea salt
½   lemon

WHAT YOU DO

1. Preheat oven to 425°F. Line a 15×10×1-inch baking pan with a silicone baking mat or parchment; set aside. In a small bowl combine garlic and ½ tsp. of the kosher salt. Using the back of a spoon, smash garlic and salt until garlic begins to release its oil; set aside.

2. Trim broccoli stems; cut stalks lengthwise into halves and/or quarters. Place in prepared baking pan. Pour garlic oil and olives over; toss well. Sprinkle with remaining ½ tsp. kosher salt. Roast 20 to 25 minutes, tossing occasionally, until tender but al dente. Transfer to a serving dish.

3. To serve, sprinkle with flaked sea salt; drizzle with additional olive oil. Squeeze lemon juice over. Makes 8 servings.

RICH BEEF STEW WITH BACON AND PLUMS

Salting the meat far ahead of cooking time—overnight, in fact—has a hydrating effect on it. The salt actually helps the cells hold onto water, making the meat juicy.

PREP 1 hour 30 minutes
ROAST 20 minutes
BAKE 2 hours 45 minutes
BAKE 20 minutes

WHAT YOU NEED

1   3½- to 4-pound well-marbled beef chuck roast
1   Tbsp. kosher salt
6   oz. thick sliced, center-cut applewood smoked bacon, cut into ½-inch pieces
3   Tbsp. olive oil
1   medium butternut squash, peeled, seeded, and cut into 1-inch pieces (about 4 cups)
2   Tbsp. unsalted butter
    Kosher salt
2   cups diced yellow onions
1   leek, white part only, split lengthwise, rinsed and then blotted dry (reserve one long inner piece), and cut crosswise into slices
3   large cloves garlic, peeled and roughly chopped (about 1 heaping Tbsp.)
2¾ cups dry red wine (such as Pinot Noir)
1   to 1½ cups chicken stock
1   stick cinnamon, broken
2   whole cloves
7   whole black peppercorns
3   fresh bay leaves (or 1 dried bay leaf)
1   Tbsp. tomato paste
¼   tsp. dried thyme
5   stems fresh parsley, leaves picked and chopped, stems reserved
1   cup pitted prunes

WHAT YOU DO

1. Trim and cut roast into 2-inch pieces. Sprinkle evenly with the 1 Tbsp. kosher salt. Cover; chill overnight.

2. Preheat oven to 450°F. Line a 15×10×1-inch baking pan with a silicone baking mat; set aside. Cook bacon in 1 Tbsp. hot olive oil over medium-low heat until browned. Transfer bacon to paper towels. Reserve 3 Tbsp. drippings in skillet.

3. Place squash on prepared pan. Add 1 Tbsp. butter and 1 Tbsp. bacon drippings. Sprinkle with salt; toss to coat. Roast 20 to 30 minutes or until tender and browned, stirring once. Cover with waxed paper; set aside. Reduce oven to 275°F.

4. Add remaining 2 Tbsp. olive oil to remaining 2 Tbsp. bacon drippings in skillet; heat over medium-high heat. Blot beef well with paper towels; add to skillet in batches, being careful not to crowd the skillet. Brown deeply on all sides. Remove; set aside.

5. Drain all but 1 tsp. fat from skillet. Add remaining 1 Tbsp. butter and onions to pan. Sprinkle with salt. Stir over medium heat, scraping up browned bits from bottom of pan. Cook 3 to 4 minutes, stirring often, just until onions begin to soften. Stir in leek slices and garlic. Sprinkle with salt. Cook 4 minutes more. Transfer to a 3-qt. baking dish; set aside. Pour wine into skillet. Bring to boiling; reduce heat. Boil gently, uncovered, until reduced by half.

6. Place beef and bacon over onions. Pour reduced wine over. Add stock to almost cover. Using kitchen string, tie cinnamon, cloves, and peppercorns in a piece of cheesecloth; tuck into beef mixture. Add bay leaves. Dollop tomato paste around beef mixture. Sprinkle with thyme. Tie together parsley stems and inner leek piece; add to beef mixture. Place parchment paper over dish. Top with a triple layer of heavy foil. Seal tightly. Place on rimmed baking sheet. Bake 2 hours. Uncover; add prunes. Cover; bake 45 minutes to an hour more or until meat is easily pierced with a knife. Uncover; skim off fat. Remove and discard cheesecloth bag and parsley stems; discard.

7. Increase oven to 350°F. Add butternut squash. Bake uncovered, 20 minutes, basting once or twice. To serve, sprinkle with parsley leaves. Makes 8 servings.

ROASTED BROCCOLI AND OLIVES

RICH BEEF STEW WITH
BACON AND PLUMS

One Dough, Five Ways

Let this hardworking recipe be the hero of the holidays! One basic dough is used to make bars, slice-and-bake cookies, even cutouts. It's almost like ... magic!

MINT-GANACHE SANDWICH COOKIES

CHAI-SPICED PINE CONES

PISTACHIO-CRANBERRY STICKS

HOW IT WORKS

The concept is simple. Here's what to do: Use one batch of dough to make Cinnamon Roll Cookies or Cherry Crumb Bars. Or use one batch to make three at once: Mint-Ganache Sandwiches, Pistachio Cranberry Sticks, and Chai-Spiced Pinecones.

VANILLA COOKIE DOUGH

Talk about getting the most from your dough! With just a few minor tweaks, you can make three completely different cookies from one batch of dough. This concept is perfect for cookie swaps when you need variety and are short on time.

START TO FINISH 10 minutes

WHAT YOU NEED

1   cup butter, softened
⅔   cup sugar
½   tsp. salt
1   egg
1   Tbsp. vanilla
2   cups all-purpose flour

WHAT YOU DO

1. In a large bowl beat butter with a mixer on medium to high 30 seconds. Add the sugar and salt. Beat on medium 2 minutes, scraping bowl as needed. Beat in egg and vanilla. Beat in flour until combined. Divide dough into three portions.

MINT-GANACHE SANDWICH COOKIES

A simple chocolate ganache made in the microwave and a stir-together powdered sugar-mint frosting provides the filling for these sandwich cookies.

PREP 25 minutes
CHILL 50 minutes
BAKE 6 minutes

WHAT YOU NEED

1 portion Vanilla Cookie Dough (recipe, page 108)
2 Tbsp. heavy cream
¼ cup miniature semisweet chocolate pieces
⅔ cup powdered sugar
1 Tbsp. butter, softened
2 tsp. milk
¼ tsp. mint extract
1 drop green food coloring

WHAT YOU DO

1. Wrap and chill one dough portion 30 to 60 minutes or until easy to handle. Preheat oven to 375°F. On a lightly floured surface roll dough to a 9-inch square. Use a pastry wheel or pizza cutter to cut dough into 1½-inch squares. Arrange dough squares 2 inches apart on an ungreased cookie sheet. Prick each several times with a fork. Bake 6 to 8 minutes or until edges are lightly browned. Cool on cookie sheet 1 minute. Remove; cool on wire racks.
2. For ganache, in a small bowl microwave cream 20 to 30 seconds or just until boiling. Add chocolate (do not stir). Let stand 5 minutes. Stir until smooth. Chill 10 minutes or until spreadable.
3. For mint frosting, in a small bowl stir together powdered sugar, butter, milk, and mint extract until spreading consistency. Add food coloring.
4. Spread frosting on the bottoms of half of the cookies. Spread ganache on bottoms of remaining cookies; chill 10 minutes to set. Top ganache-topped cookies with frosting-topped cookies. Lightly dust cookies with additional powdered sugar. Makes 18 servings.

To Store Layer filled cookies between sheets of waxed paper in an airtight container; cover. Store in the refrigerator up to 3 days or freeze up to 3 months.

CHAI-SPICED PINECONES

Sweet spices, including cardamom, ginger, cinnamon, and cloves flavor these cute pinecone cookies. Or try the Spiced Mexican Pine Cones variation featuring chili powder and cayenne and subbing pepitas for the almonds.

PREP 30 minutes
CHILL 30 minutes
BAKE 8 minutes

WHAT YOU NEED

1½ tsp. Chai Spice (recipe, below)
1 portion Vanilla Cookie Dough (recipe, page 108)
¼ cup sliced almonds
2 oz. bittersweet or semisweet chocolate, chopped
½ tsp. shortening
Powdered sugar (optional)

WHAT YOU DO

1. Stir Chai Spice into one dough portion. Wrap and chill dough 30 to 60 minutes or until easy to handle. Preheat oven to 375°F. On a lightly floured surface roll dough to ¼-inch thickness. Use a 2-inch teardrop-shape or oval cookie cutter to cut dough. Arrange cutouts 2 inches apart on an ungreased cookie sheet. Insert almonds at an angle on cutouts to resemble a pine cone, leaving about ½ inch at the bottoms.
2. Bake 8 to 10 minutes or until edges start to brown. Cool on cookie sheet 1 minute. Remove; cool on wire racks.
3. Place chocolate and shortening in a small bowl. Microwave 1 minute or until melted and smooth, stirring once. Dip the bottom of each pinecone into melted chocolate mixture. Let stand or chill until set. If desired, lightly sprinkle with powdered sugar. Makes 18 servings.

Chai Spice In a small bowl stir together 1 tsp. ground cardamom, ¼ tsp. ground ginger, ¼ tsp. ground cinnamon, and dash ground cloves.

Spiced Mexican Pine Cones Prepare as above, except omit Chai Spice. Instead, stir in 1 tsp. chili powder and dash cayenne pepper into dough. Substitute raw pepitas for the almonds.

To Store Layer cookies between sheets of waxed paper in an airtight container; cover. Store in the refrigerator up to 3 days or freeze up to 3 months.

PISTACHIO-CRANBERRY STICKS

These shortbread-style cookies are simple to shape—just roll out and cut into rectangles—and decorate. A quick dip in melted white baking pieces and a sprinkle of citrus zest and chopped pistachios and dried cranberries and they're ready to go.

PREP 25 minutes
CHILL 30 minutes
BAKE 8 minutes

WHAT YOU NEED

½ cup finely chopped pistachios
¼ cup dried cranberries, finely chopped
1 portion Vanilla Cookie Dough (recipe, page 108)
½ cup white baking pieces
1 tsp. shortening
1 tsp. tangerine or orange zest

WHAT YOU DO

1. Stir the pistachios and cranberries into one dough portion. Cover and chill dough 30 to 60 minutes or until easy to handle. Preheat oven to 375°F. On a lightly floured surface roll the dough to an 8×6-inch rectangle about ½ inch thick. Cut lengthwise into eight ¾-inch-wide strips. Cut each into thirds crosswise. Place 1 inch apart on an ungreased cookie sheet.
2. Bake 8 minutes or until edges start to brown. Cool on cookie sheet 1 minute. Remove; cool on wire racks.
3. Place baking pieces and shortening in a small bowl. Microwave 1 minute or until melted and smooth, stirring once. Dip ends of cookie sticks into melted chocolate to coat. Place on waxed paper; sprinkle white chocolate with zest and, if desired, additional finely chopped pistachios and/or dried cranberries. Let stand or chill until set. Makes 24 servings.

To Store Layer cookies between sheets of waxed paper in an airtight container; cover. Store in the refrigerator up to 3 days or freeze up to 3 months.

CINNAMON ROLL COOKIES

A swirl of cinnamon sugar and creamy icing makes these cookies taste like your favorite bakery cinnamon rolls—with a tantalizing cookie crunch.

PREP 30 minutes
CHILL 30 minutes
FREEZE 30 minutes
BAKE 8 minutes

WHAT YOU NEED

1   recipe Vanilla Cookie Dough (3 portions) (recipe, page 108)
1   egg, lightly beaten
½   cup packed brown sugar
2   tsp. ground cinnamon, apple pie spice, or pumpkin pie spice
1   recipe Cream Cheese Icing Drizzle

WHAT YOU DO

1. Wrap and chill dough 30 to 60 minutes or until easy to handle. On a floured surface roll dough to a 15×10-inch rectangle. Brush with egg. Stir together brown sugar and cinnamon and sprinkle over dough. Roll up from a long side. Place on a baking sheet or tray, cover, and freeze about 30 minutes or until firm enough to slice.

2. Preheat oven to 375°F. Line cookie sheets with parchment paper. Slice roll into ¼-inch slices. Place 2 inches apart on prepared cookie sheets. Bake 8 to 10 minutes or until edges are lightly browned. Cool on cookie sheets 1 minute. Remove; cool on wire racks. Drizzle cooled cookies with Cream Cheese Icing Drizzle. Makes 40 servings.

To Store Layer undrizzled cookies between sheets of waxed paper in an airtight container; cover. Store at room temperature up to 3 days or freeze up to 3 months. Drizzle with Cream Cheese Icing Drizzle before serving.

Cream Cheese Icing Drizzle In a medium bowl beat 2 oz. softened cream cheese and 1 Tbsp. softened butter with a mixer on medium until smooth. Beat in ¾ cup powdered sugar and enough milk (2 to 3 Tbsp.) to make drizzling consistency. Makes about ¾ cup.

CHERRY-HAZELNUT CRUMB BARS

It's easy to turn the Vanilla Cookie Dough into a bar recipe. Spread the bar with a luscious cherry-hazelnut topping and finish it with a buttery oat crumble. Magnificent? Oh, yes!

PREP 35 minutes
BAKE 45 minutes

WHAT YOU NEED

    Nonstick cooking spray
1   recipe Vanilla Cookie Dough (3 portions) (recipe, page 108)
½   cup butter, cut up
1   cup all-purpose flour
½   cup packed brown sugar
½   cup rolled oats
½   tsp. salt
½   cup hazelnuts, chopped
1   12-oz. pkg. frozen pitted dark sweet cherries (2 cups)
¾   cup pomegranate juice
¼   cup hazelnut liqueur
¼   cup honey
1   Tbsp. cornstarch

WHAT YOU DO

1. Preheat oven to 375°F. Line a 13×9-inch baking pan with foil, extending foil over the edges of the pan. Lightly coat foil with cooking spray. Using an offset spatula, spread the dough in the pan, holding the foil in place while spreading. Bake 15 minutes or just until starting to brown. Remove to a wire rack.

2. For crumb topping, in a food processor combine the butter, flour, brown sugar, oats, and salt. Cover and pulse until mixture resembles fine crumbs. Stir in the nuts. Set aside.

3. For filling, in a large saucepan combine the cherries, pomegranate juice, liqueur, and honey. Bring to boiling; reduce heat. Simmer, uncovered, 10 minutes, stirring occasionally (watch carefully because mixture foams up). Stir together cornstarch and 1 Tbsp. water. Add to cherry mixture. Cook and stir until thickened and bubbly. Spoon filling over partially baked crust. Sprinkle evenly with crumb topping.

4. Bake about 30 minutes or until topping is golden. Cool in pan on a wire rack. Use edges of foil to lift uncut bars out of pan. Transfer to a cutting board. Cut into bars or triangles. Makes 36 servings.

CINNAMON ROLL COOKIES

CHERRY-HAZELNUT
CRUMB BARS

Serve Them Soup

Some of the simplest, most satisfying foods you can feed visiting friends and relatives this season are soups—and they're easy on the cook too. These hearty soups are inspired by comfort foods in most weekly rotations—mac 'n' cheese, spaghetti, pizza, tacos—because, let's face it, they're delicious. So imagine those favorites as hot, simmering soups and stir them up this season. Everyone will love them—even the littlest houseguests.

EASY TACO SOUP

This ground beef- or turkey- (take your pick!) based soup couldn't be any simpler to make. And while it simmers in the slow cooker, you can enjoy time with family and friends.

PREP 15 minutes
SLOW COOK 6 hours on Low or 3 hours on High

WHAT YOU NEED
1 lb. ground beef or uncooked ground turkey
1 15-oz. can black-eyed peas, rinsed and drained
1 15-oz. can black beans, rinsed and drained
1 15-oz. can red kidney beans, rinsed and drained
1 15-oz. can chili beans in chili gravy, undrained
1 14.5-oz. can Mexican-style stewed tomatoes, undrained and snipped
2 14.5-oz. cans lower sodium beef broth
1 11-oz. can whole kernel corn with sweet peppers, drained
1 1.25-oz. envelope taco seasoning mix
   Toppings: shredded cheese, sliced jalapeños, chopped avocado, snipped cilantro, and/or tortilla chips (optional)

WHAT YOU DO
1. In a large skillet cook ground meat over medium-high heat until browned. Drain off fat if necessary.
2. In a 4- to 6-quart slow cooker combine meat and next eight ingredients (through taco seasoning mix).
3. Cover and cook on low 6 to 8 hours or on high 3 to 4 hours. Serve with desired toppings. Makes 8 servings.

LASAGNA SOUP

Everyone loves lasagna but the layered and baked version is time-consuming to put together. This soup features all the same flavors of this favorite food but can be on the table in just 45 minutes.

PREP 20 minutes
COOK 25 minutes

WHAT YOU NEED

- 1 lb. uncooked bulk turkey Italian sausage or lean ground beef
- ½ cup chopped onion
- ½ cup chopped green sweet pepper
- 3 cloves garlic, minced
- 4 cups reduced-sodium chicken broth
- 1 14.5-oz. can no-salt-added diced tomatoes, undrained
- 2 8-oz. cans no-salt-added tomato sauce
- 2 tsp. dried Italian seasoning, crushed
- 10 oz. whole wheat lasagna noodles, broken into bite-size pieces
- ¾ cup part-skim ricotta cheese
- 6 Tbsp. finely shredded Parmesan cheese
- 3 Tbsp. snipped fresh basil
- ¼ tsp. crushed red pepper

WHAT YOU DO

1. In a large pot cook sausage, onion, sweet pepper, and garlic over medium-high heat until sausage is browned. Drain off fat. Add the next four ingredients (through Italian seasoning). Bring to boiling; reduce heat. Simmer, covered, 20 minutes.

2. Meanwhile, cook pasta according to package directions; drain. Stir into soup.

3. To serve, spoon ricotta into six bowls. Top with soup. Stir together Parmesan, basil, and crushed red pepper. Sprinkle over soup. Makes 6 servings.

Make-Ahead Directions Prepare as directed through Step 1. Let soup cool and transfer to an airtight container; cover. Store in the refrigerator up to 2 days or freeze up to 3 months. Return soup to pot and bring to simmering. Continue as directed.

Tip For a vegetarian version, substitute 3 cups sliced fresh mushrooms for the sausage and vegetable broth for the chicken broth.

LASAGNA SOUP

ALL-AMERICAN CHEESEBURGER SOUP

Dill pickles and hot french fries make perfect sense as soup toppings when the soup is a deconstructed version of America's favorite sandwich.

PREP 20 minutes
COOK 25 minutes

WHAT YOU NEED

- 1 lb. ground beef
- ½ cup chopped onion
- ½ cup chopped celery
- 2 cloves garlic, minced
- 2 Tbsp. all-purpose flour
- 2 14.5-oz. cans lower sodium beef broth (3½ cups)
- 2 medium potatoes, coarsely chopped
- 1 14.5-oz. can diced tomatoes, drained
- 8 oz. American cheese slices, torn (about 12 slices)
- 1 6-oz. can tomato paste
- ¼ cup ketchup
- 2 Tbsp. Dijon-style mustard
- 1 cup whole milk
- 6 cocktail buns, split and toasted*
  Assorted condiments: pickles, onions, lettuce, mustard, and/or ketchup (optional)
  Hot french fries (optional)

WHAT YOU DO

1. In a large pot cook beef, onion, celery, and garlic over medium heat until meat is browned and vegetables are tender. Drain off fat. Sprinkle flour over beef mixture; cook and stir 2 minutes. Stir in broth and potatoes. Bring to boiling, stirring occasionally; reduce heat. Simmer, covered, about 10 minutes or until potatoes are tender.

2. Stir in next five ingredients (through mustard). Cook and stir until cheese is melted and soup comes to a gentle boil. Stir in milk; heat through. Top toasted buns with condiments and serve with soup. If desired, top soup with hot french fries. Makes 6 servings.

*Note To toast buns, preheat the broiler. Place split buns, cut sides up, on a broiler pan. Brush lightly with 1 Tbsp. melted butter or olive oil. Broil, 3 to 4 inches from heat, about 1 minute or until lightly toasted.

ALL-AMERICAN CHEESEBURGER SOUP

CHICKEN
POT PIE
SOUP

CHICKEN POT PIE SOUP

Homey—and a little healthier than its namesake—this creamy, veggie-packed chicken and noodle soup is top-shelf comfort food.

PREP 35 minutes
BAKE 10 minutes

WHAT YOU NEED

1   Tbsp. butter
½   cup chopped carrot
½   cup chopped celery
⅓   cup chopped onion
2   cloves garlic, minced
4   cups reduced-sodium chicken broth
2   cups chopped cooked chicken breast (about 10 oz.)
2   cups dried medium egg noodles
½   tsp. seasoned salt
½   tsp. dry mustard
½   tsp. chili powder
½   tsp. black pepper
¼   tsp. curry powder
1   cup half-and-half
1   Tbsp. all-purpose flour
1   cup chopped fresh broccoli
⅓   cup frozen peas
1   recipe Quick Biscuits

WHAT YOU DO

1. In a large saucepan melt butter over medium heat. Add carrot, celery, onion, and garlic; cook about 5 minutes or until tender, stirring occasionally. Stir in the next eight ingredients (through curry powder). Bring to boiling; reduce heat. Simmer, covered, about 10 minutes or until noodles are tender.

2. In a small bowl whisk together half-and-half and flour; gradually stir into chicken mixture. Stir in broccoli and peas. Simmer, uncovered, about 5 minutes more or until slightly thickened. Serve with Quick Biscuits. Makes 6 servings.

Quick Biscuits Preheat oven to 450°F. In a medium bowl stir together 2 cups all-purpose flour, 4 tsp. sugar, 4 tsp. baking powder, and ½ tsp. cream of tartar. Using a pastry blender, cut in ½ cup butter until mixture resembles coarse crumbs. Make a well in the center of the flour mixture. Add ⅔ cup milk all at once. Using a fork, stir just until mixture is moistened. Turn dough out onto a lightly floured surface. Knead dough by folding and gently pressing just until dough holds together. Pat into an 8-inch square. Cut into 12 rectangles; place 1 inch apart on a baking sheet. Bake 10 to 12 minutes or until golden.

SUPREME PIZZA SOUP

If you can't fathom eating anything that tastes just like pizza without the crust, be sure to serve this soup with the optional Pizza Crust Dippers.

PREP 40 minutes
COOK 20 minutes

WHAT YOU NEED

- 1   lb. bulk Italian sausage, cooked
- 2   3.5-oz. pkg. sliced pepperoni
- 2   Tbsp. olive oil
- 2   8-oz. pkg. fresh button mushrooms, coarsely chopped
- 1   cup chopped red onion
- ¾   cup chopped red sweet pepper
- ¾   cup chopped green sweet pepper
- 2   Tbsp. minced garlic
- 1   tsp. crushed red pepper
- 3   28-oz. cans diced tomatoes, undrained
- 2   14.5-oz. cans reduced-sodium chicken broth
- ½   cup pitted black olives, halved
- 1   Tbsp. dried Italian seasoning, crushed
       Grated Parmesan cheese
       Pizza Crust Dippers (optional)

WHAT YOU DO

1. In a large skillet cook sausage over medium heat about 10 minutes or until browned. Remove sausage from skillet and drain on paper towels.

2. In the same skillet cook pepperoni over medium heat about 5 minutes or until pepperoni starts to crisp, stirring occasionally. Remove from skillet and drain on paper towels.

3. Meanwhile, in an 8- to 10-qt. Dutch oven heat 1 Tbsp. olive oil over medium-low heat. Add mushrooms, red onion, and sweet peppers; cook about 10 minutes or until crisp-tender, stirring occasionally. Push vegetables aside and add the remaining 1 Tbsp. olive oil to the Dutch oven. Add garlic and crushed red pepper to the oil; cook 30 seconds or until garlic is aromatic, stirring frequently.

4. Add the sausage, the pepperoni, the tomatoes, broth, olives, and Italian seasoning to soup in the pot. Bring to boiling; reduce heat. Simmer, uncovered, 20 minutes, stirring occasionally.

5. Serve soup topped with cheese, and, if desired, with Pizza Crust Dippers. Makes 12 servings.

Pizza Crust Dippers Press one 13.8-oz. pkg. refrigerated pizza crust onto a greased baking sheet. Sprinkle with fresh rosemary and chopped garlic. Drizzle with olive oil. If desired, sprinkle with shredded Parmesan cheese. Bake according to package directions. Cut into wedges.

SPAGHETTI-LOVER'S SOUP

No rolling and shaping meatballs involved in making this family-friendly slow-cooked soup that has all the flavors of everyone's favorite Italian pasta dish.

PREP 25 minutes
COOK 8 hours on Low or 4 hours on High + 20 minutes on High

WHAT YOU NEED

- 1   lb. lean ground beef
- ½   cup chopped onion
- ½   cup chopped green sweet pepper
- ½   cup chopped celery
- ½   cup chopped carrot
- 2   cloves garlic, minced
- 2   14.5-oz. cans no-salt-added diced tomatoes, undrained
- 1   14-oz. jar spaghetti sauce
- 1   cup water
- 1   Tbsp. quick-cooking tapioca, crushed
- ½   tsp. dried Italian seasoning, crushed
- ¼   tsp. salt
- ¼   tsp. black pepper
- ⅛   tsp. cayenne pepper
- 2   oz. spaghetti, broken into 2-inch pieces

WHAT YOU DO

1. In a large skillet cook ground beef, onion, sweet pepper, celery, carrot, and garlic over medium heat until meat is browned and vegetables are tender. Drain off fat. Transfer meat mixture to a 3½- to 4-qt. slow cooker. Stir the next eight ingredients (through cayenne pepper) into meat mixture in cooker.

2. Cover and cook on low 8 to 10 hours or on high 4 to 5 hours.

3. If using low setting, turn to high. Stir in spaghetti. Cover and cook 15 to 20 minutes more or until pasta is tender. Makes 6 servings.

SUPREME PIZZA SOUP

SPAGHETTI-LOVER'S SOUP

BEEF STROGANOFF
SOUP

CHICKEN ENCHILADA SOUP

Pick up a rotisserie chicken at the supermarket and turn it into this quick-to-fix Mexican-inspired soup.

PREP 20 minutes
COOK 30 minutes

WHAT YOU NEED

1   Tbsp. vegetable oil
1   cup chopped onion
2   cloves garlic, minced
1   32-oz. carton reduced-sodium chicken broth
½   cup cornmeal
2   cups shredded cooked chicken
1   14.5-oz. can diced tomatoes, undrained
1   10-oz. can enchilada sauce
1   4-oz. can diced green chiles, undrained
1   cup shredded cheddar cheese (4 oz.)
    Fried flour tortilla strips or tortilla chips
    Snipped cilantro and/or sour cream (optional)

WHAT YOU DO

1. In a large saucepan heat oil over medium-high heat. Add onion and garlic; cook and stir 4 minutes or until onion is tender. Stir in broth and cornmeal. Bring to boiling, stirring constantly. Stir in next four ingredients (through chiles). Heat through. Stir in half of the cheese.
2. Top servings with remaining cheese and tortilla strips. If desired, serve with cilantro and/or sour cream. Makes 8 servings.

CHICKEN
ENCHILADA
SOUP

BEEF STROGANOFF SOUP

Serve this hearty and rich-tasting soup with a crisp green salad.

PREP 20 minutes
COOK 30 minutes

WHAT YOU NEED

1   lb. beef sirloin steak, trimmed and sliced into bite-size pieces
    Salt and black pepper
2   Tbsp. butter
8   oz. fresh button mushrooms, sliced
1   cup chopped onion
2   cloves garlic, minced
5   cups lower sodium beef broth
1   Tbsp. Worcestershire sauce
1   Tbsp. tomato paste
1½ cups dried egg noodles
½   cup sour cream
2   Tbsp. all-purpose flour
    Snipped fresh Italian parsley
    Sour cream (optional)

WHAT YOU DO

1. Sprinkle steak with salt and pepper. In a Dutch oven melt butter over medium-high heat. Cook steak, half at a time, in hot butter until browned. Set meat aside.
2. Add mushrooms, onion, and garlic to Dutch oven. Cook and stir over medium heat 5 to 7 minutes or until mushrooms are tender. Stir in broth, Worcestershire sauce, and tomato paste; bring to boiling. Add noodles; boil gently, uncovered, 5 to 7 minutes or until noodles are tender.
3. In a medium bowl whisk together the ½ cup sour cream and flour. Whisk 1 cup of the soup broth into sour cream mixture until smooth. Return sour cream mixture to soup. Cook and stir until thickened and bubbly. Cook and stir 1 minute more. Add meat to soup and cook just until meat is heated though. Top servings with parsley and, if desired, additional sour cream. Makes 6 servings.

GRILLED CHEESE SANDWICH SOUP

The bread in a grilled cheese takes the form of cheese-topped croutons in this soup version of the sandwich.

PREP 35 minutes
COOK 20 minutes

WHAT YOU NEED

- 2   Tbsp. butter
- ¾   cup chopped onion
- ½   cup finely chopped carrot
- 3   cloves garlic, minced
- 1   32-oz. carton reduced-sodium chicken broth
- 1   large baking potato (12 oz.), peeled and cut into 1-inch pieces
- 2   cups half-and-half
- ½   tsp. dry mustard or 1 Tbsp. Dijon-style, spicy brown, horseradish, or coarse ground mustard
- 4   oz. cream cheese, cubed and softened
- 1   lb. shredded three-cheese blend (cheddar, Colby, and Monterey Jack)
- 12 ½-inch slices baguette-style French bread
- 1   Tbsp. olive oil

WHAT YOU DO

1. In a large saucepan melt butter over medium heat. Add onion, carrot, and garlic; cook and stir 4 to 5 minutes or until vegetables are tender. Add broth and potato. Bring to boiling; reduce heat. Simmer, covered, 20 to 25 minutes or until potato is tender. Remove from heat; cool slightly.

2. Using a handheld immersion blender, blend broth mixture until smooth*. Stir in half-and-half and mustard. Remove ½ cup soup to a small bowl; stir in cream cheese until smooth. Whisk cream cheese mixture back into soup. Cook and stir over medium-low heat until heated through. Reduce heat to low. Gradually add 3 cups of the shredded cheese, whisking until cheese is melted.

3. Meanwhile, preheat broiler. Brush both sides of bread slices with oil; place on a baking sheet lined with foil. Broil 3 to 4 inches from the heat 2 to 3 minutes or until toasted, turning once. Sprinkle with the remaining 1 cup shredded cheese. If necessary, broil until cheese is melted.

4. Top each serving with cheese-topped bread slices. Makes 6 servings.

*Tip Or transfer broth mixture, about one-fourth at a time, to a blender or food processor. Remove cap from lid and hold a folded kitchen towel over opening. Cover and blend or process until smooth. Return pureed soup to saucepan.

Smoky Gouda For a smoky flavor, substitute smoked Gouda cheese for the three-cheese blend.

Spicy Pepper Jack For a spicy flavor, substitute Monterey Jack cheese with jalapeño peppers for the three-cheese blend.

Spicy Hot Pepper Sauce Add 1 to 2 tsp. bottled hot pepper sauce or Sriracha sauce to soup after cheese is melted.

Mac and Cheese Soup Stir 2 cups small broccoli florets (if desired), 2 cups cooked elbow macaroni, and 5 oz. cooked ham (cubed), into soup after the cheese is melted. Cook and stir 5 minutes (or until broccoli is tender, if using). Omit Step 3. Sprinkle servings with smoked paprika or paprika.

MAC AND CHEESE SOUP

GRILLED CHEESE SANDWICH SOUP

Quick & Easy Appetizers

Add a few extras to the grocery cart and be ready in a snap with tasty nibbles for last-minute guests.

EASY BAKE

Mix together a container of ricotta cheese, half a package of thawed and drained frozen spinach, olive oil, a sprinkle of sage, a minced garlic clove, salt, and pepper. Bake at 400°F 25 to 30 minutes. Serve with toasted baguette slices.

ON A STICK

Skewer cooked mini meatballs and tortellini, and serve with your favorite homemade or purchased marinara.

NO COOK

Wrap pears and white cheddar with prosciutto (or any combo of cheese and charcuterie).

EASY BAKE

ON A STICK

NO COOK

WHITE BEAN HUMMUS WITH ROASTED TOMATOES

Cut the pointed top from a head of garlic, leaving bulb intact while exposing individual cloves. Remove any loose papery coating. Place garlic, cut side up, in a 6-oz. custard cup. Drizzle with 1 tsp. olive oil. Cover with foil. Bake 20 to 25 minutes in a 400°F oven or until garlic is soft. Remove; let cool. Squeeze garlic cloves into a food processor. Add two 15-oz. cans cannellini beans, 1 Tbsp. lemon juice, 1 Tbsp. olive oil, and ½ tsp. salt. Process to desired consistency. Top with roasted cherry tomatoes.

MINT AVOCADO DIP

Place 2 ripe pitted avocados and 2 Tbsp. lime juice in a medium bowl; coarsely mash with a potato masher or fork. Stir in ¼ cup fresh mint leaves, 3 thinly sliced green onions, and ¼ tsp. salt. Transfer to a serving bowl. Serve immediately or cover surface with plastic wrap and chill up to 24 hours. If desired, garnish with additional mint just before serving.

SMOKY BLUE CHEESE DIP

Place 1 clove garlic on a cutting board; sprinkle with ¼ tsp. salt. Use the side of a chef's knife to smear salt and garlic together until a paste forms. Transfer to a medium bowl. Whisk in 2 tsp. white wine vinegar. Stir in 6 oz. plain Greek yogurt, ¼ cup mayonnaise, a pinch of smoked paprika, and a pinch of pepper. Fold in 8 oz. crumbled blue cheese.

WHITE BEAN HUMMUS WITH ROASTED TOMATOES

SMOKY BLUE CHEESE DIP

MINT AVOCADO DIP

NEW WAYS WITH PUFF PASTRY

'Tis the season for grazing. Whip up a little something quickly with frozen pastry.

CURRIED POTATO TARTS

Cut thawed puff pastry into 2½-inch squares; press into mini muffin tins. Fill pastry cups with a mix of mashed potatoes, peas, and curry powder. Bake at 400°F 25 minutes. Sprinkle with cilantro.

APPLE-CHEDDAR BITES

Cut a sheet of thawed puff pastry into 2-inch squares. Prick with a fork, then spread a bit of apple butter in the center of each square. Top with shredded cheddar. Bake at 350°F 18 minutes.

gifts

SPREAD GOOD CHEER
Make the holidays more
meaningful by giving
presents infused with your
time, talent, and love.

Good Taste Gifts

Whip up delights for your favorite foodies with creative gifts they'll put to good use while hosting.

CUSTOM COASTERS

Metallic marking pens give a high-shine update to basic slate coasters. Create a mix-and-match set using the geometric patterns shown here (patterns on page 158) or freehand one-of-a-kind designs. Paint the coaster edges with acrylic paint; let dry. To use patterns, trace desired patterns; cut out. Using white transfer paper, place chalky side down on the face of the coaster. Top with pattern, printed side up. Tape in place and use a ballpoint pen to trace the pattern onto the slate, as shown in Photo A. Remove pattern and transfer paper and retrace lines with a metallic permanent marker. Draw designs on the coasters using oil-base paint marking pens, as shown in Photo B.

CARRY ON

Make this year's signature vino stand out from other bottles with its own handmade bag. Any color combo of felt will work—the one shown here touts similar neutrals with a pop of color at the base to be used for wine-toting all year long.

WHAT YOU NEED
Cardstock
Medium-weight chipboard
Crafts felt
Fabric glue
Hot-glue gun and glue sticks
High-density felt
Masking tape
Medium-length straight upholstery
    needle
Embroidery floss
Large cutting mat
Rotary cutting tool

WHAT YOU DO
1. Draw a 3¾-inch circle on cardstock and cut out. Trace a 3½-inch circle onto medium-weight chipboard and cut out. Trace the larger circle onto colorful crafts felt and cut out, then use fabric glue to adhere the chipboard to the center of the felt circle. Cut triangles around the fabric circle to remove bulk, and use a hot-glue gun to secure the folded felt to the chipboard, as shown in Photo A.
2. Cut an 11×12-inch piece of high-density felt and roll into a tube. Tape the tube shape while you hand-stitch the seam with upholstery needle and embroidery floss. Use the pattern, a cutting mat, and a rotary cutting tool to cut out the strap and supporting bottom piece, as shown in Photo B.
3. Assemble the three pieces as shown in Photo C, by hot-gluing the back of the colorful felt circle to the circular part of the strap. Insert a wine bottle into the tube for support and to hold in place while drying. Run a bead of hot glue along the strap where it will attach to the tube and around the circular bottom; adhere to the felt tube, positioning the strap to cover the vertical seam. Glue together the strap ends at the top to create the handle.

Stitch a large X in a contrasting color of floss as a finishing touch.

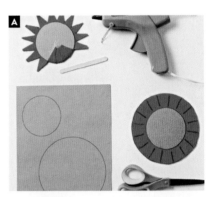

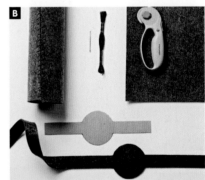

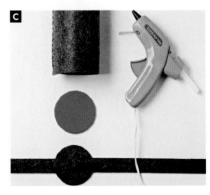

MASTER MUDDLER

One French rolling pin equals two perfect-size muddlers. A chic gold "handle" and pretty purple beet stain makes this muddler display-worthy on any bar.

WHAT YOU NEED
French rolling pin
Miter box or chop saw
Sandpaper in 150, 220, and 400-grit
Beets
Blender
Mesh strainer
1-inch foam brushes
Painters tape
Clear matte medium
Metallic acrylic paint
Boos Blocks Mystery Oil and Boos Blocks
 Board Cream

WHAT YOU DO
1. Cut the rolling pin to about 8½ inches long and use 150-grit sandpaper to smooth the cut edge. Follow with 220-grit sandpaper to lightly sand the entire surface, then sand with 400 grit until very smooth, as shown in Photo A.
2. To make the stain, cut three medium-size red beets into 1-inch pieces, place in saucepan, cover with about 2 inches of water, and bring to a boil. Reduce heat and simmer 1 hour. Blend resulting mix until it's a thick slurry, then pour beet pulp through a fine-mesh strainer. Let cool. Apply the beet liquid to the wood with a foam brush, as shown in Photo B, saturating the grain on the cut end. Allow to dry at least 1 hour, then sand with 400-grit sandpaper. Reapply stain to achieve desired color.
3. Wrap painters tape around the muddler where you want the painted handle to start then apply an even coat of clear matte medium over the surface you will paint. Apply four or five coats of metallic acrylic paint with a foam brush (allow to dry between coats). Remove tape and seal entire muddler with Boos Blocks Mystery Oil. Allow to dry overnight, then apply a coat of Boos Blocks Board Cream, as shown in Photo C.

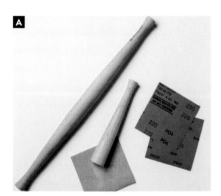

SHORTBREAD BOURBON-VANILLA COOKIE BUTTER
Recipe on page 131

Delightful Blends

Wrap delicious creations from the kitchen with lovingly made accents that display the spirit of the season.

BURLAP WRAP

Natural burlap creates a casual wrap for a squat canning jar and its lid. Remove the lid insert and cut burlap to fit. Place clear double-sided tape to the center of the lid insert to hold the burlap circle in place. Hot-glue a small cluster of mini pinecones, faux berries, and a ribbon bow to the center. Cut burlap to fit the jar. Remove a thread or two along each long edge to fray. Pull and remove three or four threads from the center of the burlap piece. Weave ¼-inch-wide grosgrain ribbon through the center of the burlap, over three threads, then under three threads until the piece is entirely woven. Place burlap sleeve around jar and knot ribbon ends.

BEST-DRESSED BATCH

Cold brew becomes an extra-special gift with the addition of a pretty bow and wooden snowflake tag. Paint a wooden snowflake with red paint using cross-hatch brushstrokes; let dry. Print a small circle with "Baby It's Cold Outside!" to fit the center of the snowflake; cut out and adhere using a glue stick. Wrap a silver chenille stem around a small round object, such as a pill bottle, to shape it into a ring to fit around printed circle. Trim chenille stem and hot-glue it in place. Drill a hole in the top of the snowflake, thread with chenille stem, and attach it to the ribbon bow.

COLD BREW COFFEE
Recipe on page 135

GINGERBREAD COOKIE BUTTER

PREP 15 minutes
STAND 45 minutes

WHAT YOU NEED

½	cup milk
3	Tbsp. coconut oil or vegetable oil
1	Tbsp. packed brown sugar
½	tsp. pumpkin pie spice
⅛	tsp. salt
8	to 9 oz. gingersnaps or speculoos cookies, coarsely broken
½	tsp. vanilla

WHAT YOU DO

1. In a large saucepan heat and stir the first five ingredients (through salt) over medium heat until milk is warm and brown sugar is dissolved. Stir in cookies; let stand 15 minutes. Transfer to a food processor or blender; add vanilla. Cover and process or blend until smooth, stopping to scrape container as needed.
2. Store in the refrigerator up to 2 weeks. Let stand at room temperature 30 minutes before serving.
Tip Serve on lemon-nut bread or scones.

VANILLA COFFEE CREAMER

Make sure to use fresh dairy products when making the creamers.

START TO FINISH 10 minutes

WHAT YOU NEED

2	cups heavy cream, half-and-half, or milk*
1	14-oz. can sweetened condensed milk
2	tsp. vanilla

WHAT YOU DO

In a 1-qt. canning jar combine all of the ingredients; seal. Store in the refrigerator up to 2 weeks. Shake before serving.
Chocolate Coffee Creamer Prepare as directed, except add 3 Tbsp. chocolate-flavor syrup. Reduce vanilla to 1 tsp. Makes about 3½ cups.
Amaretto Coffee Creamer Prepare as directed, except add 1 tsp. almond extract and ½ tsp. ground cinnamon. Omit vanilla. Makes 3¼ cups.
Caramel Coffee Creamer Prepare as directed, except add ¼ cup caramel-flavor ice cream topping. Reduce vanilla to 1 tsp. Makes 3½ cups.
Spiced Pumpkin Coffee Creamer Prepare as directed, except add 3 Tbsp. canned pumpkin and 1 tsp. pumpkin pie spice. Reduce vanilla to 1 tsp. Makes about 3½ cups.
Hazelnut Coffee Creamer Prepare as directed, except substitute 2 tsp. hazelnut extract for the vanilla. Makes 3¼ cups.
Eggnog Coffee Creamer Prepare as directed, except add 2 tsp. rum extract and ½ tsp. ground nutmeg. Reduce vanilla to 1 tsp. Makes 3¼ cups.
French Vanilla Coffee Creamer Prepare as directed, except substitute 2 tsp. vanilla bean paste for the vanilla. Makes 3¼ cups.
*Tip If you prefer, use nondairy milk, such as soy, coconut, or almond milk.

GINGERBREAD COOKIE BUTTER

VANILLA COFFEE
CREAMER

GINGERBREAD JARS
Mini gingerbread ornaments, available in crafts stores, dress up a plain container in a jiffy. Layer two contrasting narrow ribbons and slip them through an ornament loop. Tie the ribbons around the container.

BUTTONED-UP TIGHT
Wide-mouth jars come in all sizes to hold just the amount of desired creamer. Cut a white paper cuff to fit the jar and use double-sided tape to hold it in place. Add a layer of decorative paper and a row of buttons, as shown in the photograph. A circle of decorative paper, inserted between the jar rim and lid, completes the packaging.

SALTED CARAMEL SAUCE
Recipe on page 131

STACKED FOR SMILES

A pair of rounded jars, one for caramel and one for sea salt, works perfectly for gifting this recipe. Use black glass paint to make simple snowman eyes and mouth; let dry. Hot-glue a red bead nose to the face and a snowflake trim to the top of the lid. From black felt, cut a donut-shape hat brim approximately 1 inch larger than the lid. Place the caramel and salt in their respective jars. Use adhesive foam to hold the small jar in the center of the large jar lid. Pull the hat brim onto the lid. Cut a piece of ribbon for the scarf, wrap around the small jar, cross over the ends, and use a dot of hot glue to tack the ribbon together. Hot-glue a snowflake trim to the scarf.

ONE OF A GRIND

No need to wrap this pretty grinder; a clever tag is all that's needed. Write "'Tis the Seasoning!" on a cardstock tag and tie it onto the grinder using two colors of bakers string.

PRAIRIE SEASONING
Recipe on page 131

SALTED CARAMEL SAUCE

PREP 15 minutes
COOL 2 hours

WHAT YOU NEED
¾ cup packed brown sugar
½ cup butter, cut up
½ cup heavy cream
3 Tbsp. light-color corn syrup
1 tsp. vanilla
½ tsp. sea salt or kosher salt

WHAT YOU DO
1. In a 2-qt. heavy saucepan combine the first four ingredients (through corn syrup). Bring to boiling over medium-high heat, stirring to dissolve sugar and melt butter. Reduce heat to medium. Boil, uncovered, at a steady rate 5 minutes (do not stir). Remove from heat; stir in vanilla.
2. Transfer sauce to a small heatproof bowl. Cover and cool 2 hours (sauce will thicken as it cools). Before serving, sprinkle with salt.
To Store Store in the refrigerator up to 1 week. If desired, heat until warm before using.

PRAIRIE SEASONING

START TO FINISH 15 minutes

WHAT YOU NEED
2 Tbsp. fennel seeds
3 Tbsp. coarse sea salt
3 Tbsp. dried minced onion
2 Tbsp. whole pink peppercorns
2 Tbsp. dried minced garlic
2 Tbsp. dried parsley
1 Tbsp. dried celery
1 Tbsp. dried lavender
1 Tbsp. freeze-dried chives

WHAT YOU DO
1. Preheat a small dry skillet over medium heat. Add fennel seeds; shake skillet and heat 30 seconds or just until toasted and fragrant. Transfer to a small bowl; cool.
2. Stir in the remaining ingredients. Transfer mixture to a grinder mill.

PACIFIC SEASONING

START TO FINISH 10 minutes

WHAT YOU NEED
3 Tbsp. coriander seeds
⅓ cup whole star anise, crushed
3 Tbsp. coarse sea salt
3 Tbsp. dried minced onion
3 Tbsp. whole black peppercorns
3 Tbsp. whole Szechwan peppercorns
2 Tbsp. dried parsley
1 Tbsp. dried orange zest
12 whole cloves

WHAT YOU DO
1. Preheat a small dry skillet over medium heat. Add coriander seeds; shake skillet and heat 30 to 60 seconds or just until toasted and fragrant. Transfer to a small bowl; cool.
2. Stir in the remaining ingredients. Transfer mixture to a grinder mill.

EVERYDAY SEASONING

START TO FINISH 10 minutes

WHAT YOU NEED
2 Tbsp. coriander seeds
¼ cup smoked coarse sea salt
¼ cup dried minced garlic
¼ cup whole black peppercorns
2 Tbsp. dried minced onion
2 Tbsp. crushed red pepper
2 Tbsp. dried parsley
2 Tbsp. freeze-dried chives
4 tsp. dried rosemary

WHAT YOU DO
1. Preheat a small dry skillet over medium heat. Add coriander seeds; shake skillet and heat 30 to 60 seconds or just until toasted and fragrant. Transfer to a small bowl; cool.
2. Stir in the remaining ingredients. Transfer mixture to a grinder mill.

CITRUS SEASONING

START TO FINISH 10 minutes

WHAT YOU NEED
3 Tbsp. yellow mustard seeds
⅓ cup coarse sea salt
⅓ cup whole black peppercorns
3 Tbsp. dried minced garlic
3 Tbsp. dried minced onion
3 Tbsp. dried tarragon, crushed
3 Tbsp. dried parsley
1 Tbsp. dried lemon zest
1 Tbsp. dried orange zest

WHAT YOU DO
1. Preheat a small dry skillet over medium heat. Add mustard seeds; shake skillet and heat 30 to 60 seconds or just until toasted and fragrant. Transfer to a small bowl; cool.
2. Stir in the remaining ingredients. Transfer mixture to a grinder mill.

SHORTBREAD BOURBON-VANILLA COOKIE BUTTER

PREP 10 minutes
STAND 15 minutes

WHAT YOU NEED
½ cup milk
1 Tbsp. sugar
1 Tbsp. bourbon (optional)
1 10-oz. package shortbread cookies, coarsely crushed
1 Tbsp. vanilla bean paste

WHAT YOU DO
1. In a medium saucepan heat and stir the first three ingredients (through bourbon) over medium heat until milk is warm and sugar is dissolved. Stir in cookies; let stand 15 minutes.
2. Transfer mixture to a food processor or blender. Add vanilla bean paste. Cover and process or blend until smooth, stopping to scrape container as needed. Store in the refrigerator up to 2 weeks.
Tip Scoop onto hot waffles, cobblers, or sautéed apple slices. Layer between graham crackers when making s'mores.

MERRY MESSENGERS

Even last-minute gifts look beautiful with the addition of dimensional stickers and ribbon. Shop the scrapbook section at crafts stores to choose stickers to fit the jar. Trim the jar top with ribbon secured with a knot.

COARSE GROUND MUSTARD

PREP 15 minutes
STAND 24 hours

WHAT YOU NEED

⅔   cup white wine vinegar
⅓   cup yellow mustard seeds
⅓   cup brown mustard seeds
½   tsp. salt
½   tsp. ground ginger
⅛   tsp. ground allspice
3   Tbsp. honey
2   cloves garlic, minced

WHAT YOU DO

1. In a medium bowl combine the first six ingredients (through allspice). Cover and let stand 24 hours (seeds will absorb the liquid).

2. Transfer mustard seed mixture to a blender or food processor; add honey and garlic. Cover and blend or process 1 to 2 minutes or until desired texture and consistency (mixture will not get completely smooth), stopping to scrape container as needed.

3. Spoon mustard into four 4-ounce canning jars or airtight containers. For best flavor, chill 1 to 2 days before serving. Store in the refrigerator up to 3 months.

Creole Mustard Prepare as directed in Step 1, except stir ¼ tsp. cayenne pepper into mustard seed mixture with the spices. Continue as directed in Step 2, except reduce honey to 1 Tbsp. and add 2 to 3 tsp. prepared horseradish to mixture before blending.

Cranberry Mustard Prepare as directed in Step 1, except substitute red wine vinegar for the white wine vinegar and stir ½ tsp. cracked black pepper into mustard seed mixture with the spices. Continue as directed in Step 2, except omit honey. In a small saucepan bring ½ cup fresh or frozen cranberries and ⅓ cup pure maple syrup to boiling; reduce heat. Simmer, uncovered, 5 minutes or until berries pop. Add cranberry mixture to mustard seed mixture before blending.

COARSE GROUND
MUSTARD

**EVERYTHING
CRACKER CRISPS**
Recipe on page 135

TIN TOPPERS

Wooden pieces, painted and trimmed with metallic chenille stems, make merry knobs for holiday tins. Choose a rounded finial or tree shape and paint as desired using the photograph as a guide. Wearing protective eyeware, drill a hole in the center of the lid and in the bottom of the painted wood piece. Twist a wood screw through the underside of the lid then into the wood piece.

BERRIED BOTTLES

Long-neck bottles leave room for decoration without getting in the way of pouring. For a colorful base, hot-glue wide ribbon around the bottle neck. Wire together a small arrangement of pinecones, berries, and faux leaves, then tie to the bottle with narrow ribbon.

VANILLA EXTRACT
Recipe on page 135

VANILLA EXTRACT

PREP 10 minutes
STAND 1 month

WHAT YOU NEED
½ cup bourbon, vodka, brandy, or rum
2 vanilla beans, split lengthwise and cut into small pieces

WHAT YOU DO
1. In an 8-oz. glass jar combine liquor and vanilla bean pieces (make sure the vanilla pieces are submerged in the liquor). Cover and let stand in a cool, dark place at least 1 month, shaking jar once a week to distribute flavor. (Taste the extract after 1 month; for a stronger flavor, let it stand longer.)
2. To use, strain the extract through a fine-mesh sieve lined with two layers of 100%-cotton cheesecloth to remove pieces of vanilla beans. Or, if making Vanilla Extract, leave the pieces of vanilla in the extract to continue to develop flavor.
3. Transfer extract to a bottle; seal. Store in a cool, dark place up to 1 year.

Cherry Extract Prepare as directed, using vodka, brandy, or rum for the liquor, and substitute ½ cup pitted fresh dark sweet cherries for the vanilla beans.

Chocolate Extract Prepare as directed, except use vodka, brandy, or rum for the liquor and substitute ¼ cup cacao nibs, finely crushed, for the vanilla beans. Use to flavor frostings and beverages.

Cinnamon Extract Prepare as directed, except use vodka, brandy, or rum for the liquor and substitute 3 (3-inch) cinnamon sticks, crushed, for the vanilla beans. Use for baking and to flavor frosting and beverages.

Coffee Extract Prepare as directed, except use vodka, brandy, or rum for the liquor and substitute ¼ cup coffee beans, finely crushed, for the vanilla beans. Use for baking and to flavor frosting and beverages.

Lemon Extract Remove zest from 1 large lemon, avoiding the bitter white pith. Prepare as directed, using vodka for the liquor, and substitute the lemon zest for the vanilla beans.

Mint Extract Prepare as directed, using vodka for the liquor, and substitute ½ cup packed fresh mint leaves for the vanilla beans.

Orange Extract Remove zest from 1 large orange, avoiding the bitter white pith. Prepare as directed, using vodka for the liquor, and substitute the orange zest for the vanilla beans.

Tip To crush a flavoring easily, place it in a large resealable plastic bag and crush with a meat mallet or rolling pin.

COLD BREW COFFEE

PREP 5 minutes
STAND 12 hours to 24 hours

WHAT YOU NEED
1½ cups coarsely ground coffee
6 cups cold water
Coffee creamer or milk (optional)

WHAT YOU DO
1. In a 2-qt. pitcher or glass jar stir together ground coffee and the water. Cover with plastic and let steep at room temperature 12 to 24 hours.
2. Line a fine-mesh sieve with cheesecloth or a coffee filter; pour steeped coffee through the sieve into a large bowl or another 2-qt. container. To serve, pour coffee over ice and, if desired, stir in coffee creamer or milk. (We like 1 to 2 Tbsp. to every ½ cup of cold brew, but there are no rules on ratios for coffee to water or for adding creamers or milk.) Store the remaining cold brew in the refrigerator up to 2 weeks.

EVERYTHING CRACKER CRISPS

PREP 30 minutes
STAND 30 minutes
BAKE 8 minutes per batch at 450°F

WHAT YOU NEED
¼ cup sesame seeds
¼ cup poppy seeds
2 Tbsp. dried minced garlic, crushed
2 Tbsp. dried minced onion, crushed
1¼ cups all-purpose flour
1 cup whole wheat flour
1½ tsp. baking powder
1½ tsp. salt
3 Tbsp. vegetable oil
¾ cup plus 3 Tbsp. water

WHAT YOU DO
1. In a small dry skillet stir both seeds over medium heat 1 to 2 minutes or until toasted. Remove from heat. Stir in garlic and onion; cool.
2. In a large bowl combine the next four ingredients (through salt); stir in seed mixture and oil. Add the water; stir just until moistened. Turn dough out onto a lightly floured surface and knead five times or until smooth. Divide dough into eight portions. Cover and let rest 30 minutes.
3. Preheat oven to 450°F. Line a baking sheet with parchment paper. Roll one portion of dough at a time into an 11×5-inch rectangle; transfer to prepared baking sheet. Bake 8 minutes or until brown and crisp, turning once halfway through. Remove; cool on a wire rack. Break into irregular shapes. Store at room temperature up to 5 days.

Picture It

Serve up holiday joy and memories by using photographs to make personal one-of-a-kind gifts.

TOO-SWEET TAGS

Photo tags make family gift exchanges extra fun. Print digital photos onto cardstock, then trim into rectangles and snip the top corners at angles. Or purchase chipboard tags with complex shapes and use them as templates for tracing and trimming printed tags. Punch a hole through the tag top and thread with twine or ribbon.

BOTTLED UP

Give new purpose to vintage bottles by making personalized photo gifts. Gently roll and insert a print into a glass vessel. Use the eraser end of a pencil to adjust the print through the bottle neck. Add sprigs of greenery inside the vessels and tie twine around bottle necks for natural flourishes.

FROSTY FLOATING FRAMES

So sleek, these modern frames will be appreciated by anyone on your holiday gift list.

WHAT YOU NEED

Two same-size pieces of polycarbonate with protective paper attached
Drill and ¼-inch drill bit
Photo
Glue dots
Colorful duct tape
Crafts knife
4-mm copper beading chain
4-mm copper jump rings

WHAT YOU DO

1. Tape pieces of polycarbonate together. At each top corner, make a mark ¼ inch from top edge and ½ inch from side edge. Starting slowly, drill holes as shown in Photo A. Remove tape.

2. Peel paper from one side of one piece of polycarbonate, wipe clean. Center photo on polycarbonate with glue dots. Peel paper from one side of second piece of polycarbonate, wipe clean, and place over photo.

3. Adhere duct tape to each side edge, trim flush as shown in Photo B. Peel off paper.

4. Thread chain through holes and secure with jump rings.

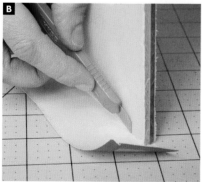

Puttin' on the Ritz

HAVE A BALL

Decked in coral and red party store pom-poms and confetti-ish sequins, a sprightly present puts a fresh face on seasonal style. A white backdrop lets you add fun forms in varying hues.

MERRY MEDALLION

Resembling a major award, a drink coaster sports a merry motif and glittery ribbon tails. It provides a prize-worthy profile atop a gift wrapped with simple white paper and gold-edged ribbon.

BEADED SNOWFLAKE BAUBLE

Two papers (one with snowlike paint spatters) and a hand-beaded trim, say you really care. Use like-color wood and bone beads for an understated look or go bold with colorful metallic beads.

ALL THAT GLITTERS

An hourglass shape, formed from glitter paper triangles edged with green and gold washi tape, proves that all that glitters is truly gift-wrapping gold. Complete the wrap with ribbon and a pair of white-edged pinecones.

SEASONAL GREENS

Organic references (linen paper, a berry pick, and cotton ribbon) complement a stamped-in-place holly sprig. Create a harmonizing gift tag by stamping on a message that expresses seasonal wishes.

kids

TIME FOR CREATIVITY

Spend time with your little ones while making unforgettable memories and joyous holiday decorations.

Beaded Beauties

Kids will love making these beaded projects that are as pretty as stained glass. Made from pony beads, melted in the oven, each of these decorations is one of a kind.

COLORFUL CANDLE PLATE

Add a little sparkle below the candle's flicker. Using a tart pan as a form, fill with a single layer of red, pink, and clear translucent pony beads. Place the pan in a 300°F oven until melted flat. Let cool and remove from pan.

STAR BRIGHT TREE TOPPER

A little one will glow with pride when the grand finale is placed on the tree top. To make the star, use an oversize star cookie cutter. Place the cookie cutter on a baking pan. Sprinkle the center with dark and light orange translucent pony beads. Complete filling the cookie cutter with yellow and clear beads. Place the tray in the oven at 300°F. Leave the tray in the oven until the beads melt flat. Remove from oven and let cool; remove star from cookie cutter. Hot-glue a skewer to the star back. Wire the skewer onto the tree to hold it in place.

PACKAGE INITIALS

Lumpy letters identify holiday gifts now and become tree ornaments later. Using a letter cookie cutter as a form, place it on a cookie sheet and fill it with a mix of translucent and opaque pony beads in similar colors. Place the pan in a 300°F oven until melted together, allowing it to be textural. Let the beads cool and remove from cookie cutter. Drill a hole in the top of the letter and thread with cord.

FRIENDLY FOREST

Placed in a window, bead-filled cookie cutters shine like Christmas lights. To make a tree, choose a tree-shape cookie cutter. Place the cookie cutter on a baking pan and fill with translucent pony beads in green and clear; blend in additional colors as desired. Place the tray in the oven at 300°F. Leave the tray in the oven until the beads melt flat. Remove from oven and let cool.

COOKIE CUTTER ORNAMENTS

Shiny beaded trims reflect the glow of Christmas lights. To make an ornament, choose a cookie cutter. Place the cookie cutter shape on a baking pan and fill with translucent pony beads, placing colors in rows if desired. To make placement easier, use a toothpick to arrange the beads. Place the tray in the oven at 300°F. Leave the tray in the oven until the beads melt flat. Remove from oven and let cool. Remove the cookie cutter. Drill a hole in the top of the ornament for hanging.

Colorful Christmas

Young ones (and you too!) will have fun discovering new ways to make holiday trims using a vivid palette of waxy crayons.

COLOR-DRENCHED EVERGREENS

Make one-of-a-kind holiday trees that share the magic of the full-size version.

WHAT YOU NEED
Pencil
Tracing paper
Scissors
Stiffened white felt
Crayons in two shades of green, red,
    orange, yellow, blue, and two shades
    of brown
Waxed paper
Pencil sharpener

WHAT YOU DO

1. Trace the tree pattern on page 158 onto paper; cut out. To make a pair of ornaments, trace around the pattern twice onto stiffened white felt, as shown in Photo A. Cut out the shapes. Cut two 1×2-inch pieces for trunks.

2. Use a pencil sharpener to make shavings from each color of crayon, as shown in Photo B.

3. Place the felt tree shapes on a piece of waxed paper and sprinkle with the two shades of green crayons, as shown in Photo C.

4. Add yellow and orange shavings at the top and some colored shavings between the green ones, as shown in Photo D.

5. Carefully place a piece of waxed paper on top of the tree shapes. Ask an adult for help and press the trees carefully with an iron, as shown in Photo E. This will take just seconds—the wax melts quickly. Peel off the waxed paper, as shown in Photo F.

6. Place the felt stump shapes on a piece of waxed paper. Sprinkle shavings from the both of the brown crayons onto the trunks, as shown in Photo G. Carefully place a piece of waxed paper on top of the tree trunks. Ask an adult for help and press the trunks carefully with an iron. Remove the waxed paper.

7. Hold a crayon-embellished tree shape over a plain piece of stiffened felt and trim a narrow border using pinking shears, as shown in Photo H.

8. Slip the end of a trunk piece between the colored tree and the backing piece; hot-glue together.

9. Using a needle and thread, stitch through the top of the tree to make a hanging loop.

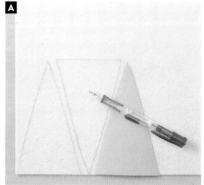

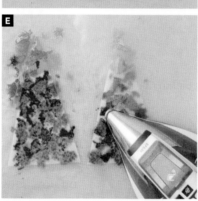

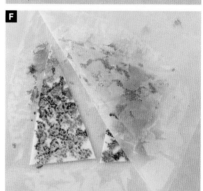

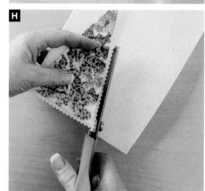

SCRIBBLE WRAP

Kids of all ages can join in the fun of making all the giftwrap for the season. Arm them with heavy white paper and a fistful of crayons then let the scribbling, doodling, and drawing begin. If desired, use a pencil sharpener to make shavings from crayons and sprinkle onto the paper; cover with waxed paper and gently iron until the wax is melted into the paper.

SNOW-FLURRY FRIEND

A basic snowman shape stands out boldly against a mix of bright crayon flecks and blotches.

WHAT YOU NEED

Artist canvas
Round lids
Crayons in black and a variety of colors
Pencil sharpener
Hair dryer

WHAT YOU DO

1. Use a black crayon to draw around two lids to make a snowman shape, as shown in Photo A. Draw a hat, as shown in Photo B.
2. Make crayon shavings from black crayon using a pencil sharpener. Sprinkle the shavings inside the hat lines, as shown in Photo C. Heat the shavings using a hair dryer, holding it far enough away so as not to blow away the shavings, as shown in Photo D. Heat until the crayon is adhered to the canvas.

3. Ask an adult to cut off black crayon slices for the eyes, buttons, and an orange chunk for nose. Heat until the crayon adheres to the canvas, as shown in Photos E and F.
4. Break off some thicker pieces of crayon to make the scarf as shown in Photo G.
5. Use the pencil sharpener to make shavings in a variety of colors; sprinkle around the snowman, as shown in Photo H. Heat until the crayon adheres to canvas, as shown in Photo I. Using the tip of a black crayon, draw on a smiley mouth.

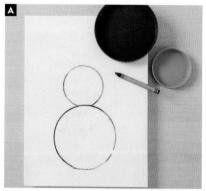

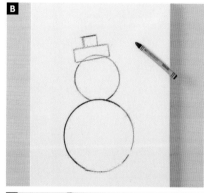

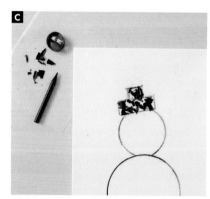

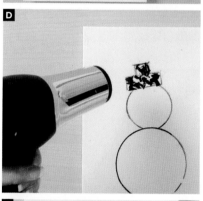

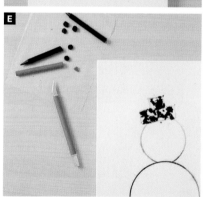

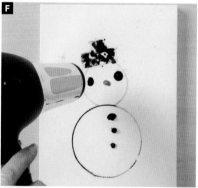

Drinking Straw Ta-Da

WHIMSICAL WREATH CARD

Layered scrapbook papers beautifully frame a tiny textural wreath. Cut a 6×12-inch piece of white cardstock; fold in half with narrow ends together. Trim the card front with a 6-inch square of patterned paper, a 5-inch square of colored cardstock, and a 4¾-inch square of white. Use glue stick to adhere the squares to the card front. Cut several 1½- to 2-inch segments from green-and-white stripe paper straws. Hot-glue the straw pieces into a ring on the card front. Tie a small ribbon bow and glue it onto the wreath.

STRIPED EASELS

Guide guests to their places at the table with mini masterpieces. Cut small rectangles of white cardstock; add dimensional letters to spell guests names on each rectangle. To make an easel, fold a straw in half. Cut a second straw in half. Pinch the end of one straw half and glue it inside the fold of the first straw. Hot-glue the horizontal piece to the front legs of the easel.

PINSTRIPE FAVORS

Treat cups get a playful coat with snippets of striped paper drinking straws lining the edge. Use hot glue to attach the straw pieces in place. Line the cups with tissue paper and fill with candy.

TREE CUPCAKE TOPPERS

Give holiday cupcakes a festive finish. Trace the pattern on page 158; cut out. Use the pattern to cut the tree shape from cardstock. Hot-glue straw pieces horizontally on the tree shape, trimming as needed to fit. Top the tree with a pom-pom and add a straw tree trunk long enough to poke into the cupcake.

SWIRLING SNOWFLAKES

Lightweight and colorful, straw snowflakes spin and float in the breeze. To connect pieces, pinch the area flat where the straws will overlap; hot-glue pieces together. Add pom-pom accents where desired. To hang, use a quilting pin to pierce through the straw top. Thread a needle and poke through holes in straw to make a loop for hanging.

patterns

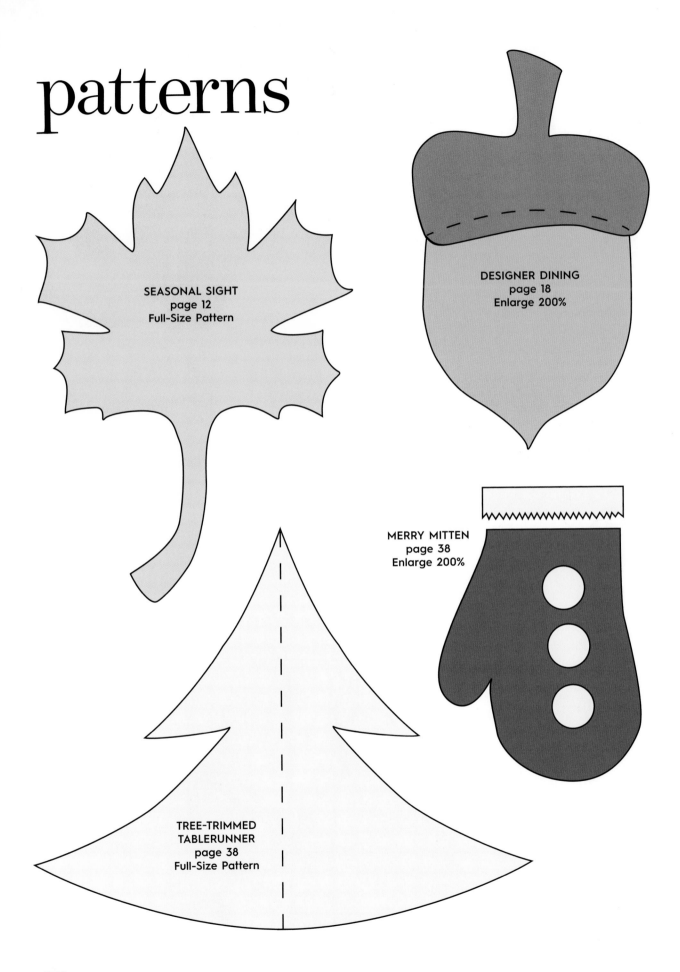

SEASONAL SIGHT
page 12
Full-Size Pattern

DESIGNER DINING
page 18
Enlarge 200%

MERRY MITTEN
page 38
Enlarge 200%

TREE-TRIMMED
TABLERUNNER
page 38
Full-Size Pattern

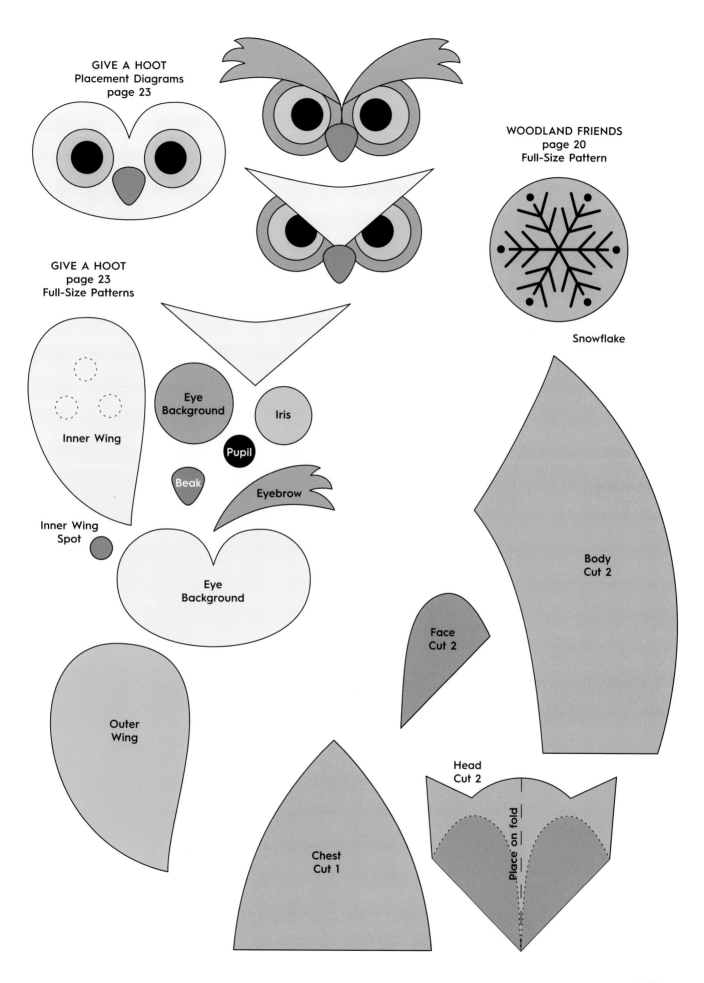

GIVE A HOOT
Placement Diagrams
page 23

WOODLAND FRIENDS
page 20
Full-Size Pattern

Snowflake

GIVE A HOOT
page 23
Full-Size Patterns

Inner Wing

Eye
Background

Iris

Pupil

Beak

Eyebrow

Inner Wing
Spot

Eye
Background

Body
Cut 2

Outer
Wing

Face
Cut 2

Chest
Cut 1

Head
Cut 2

Place on fold

Patterns

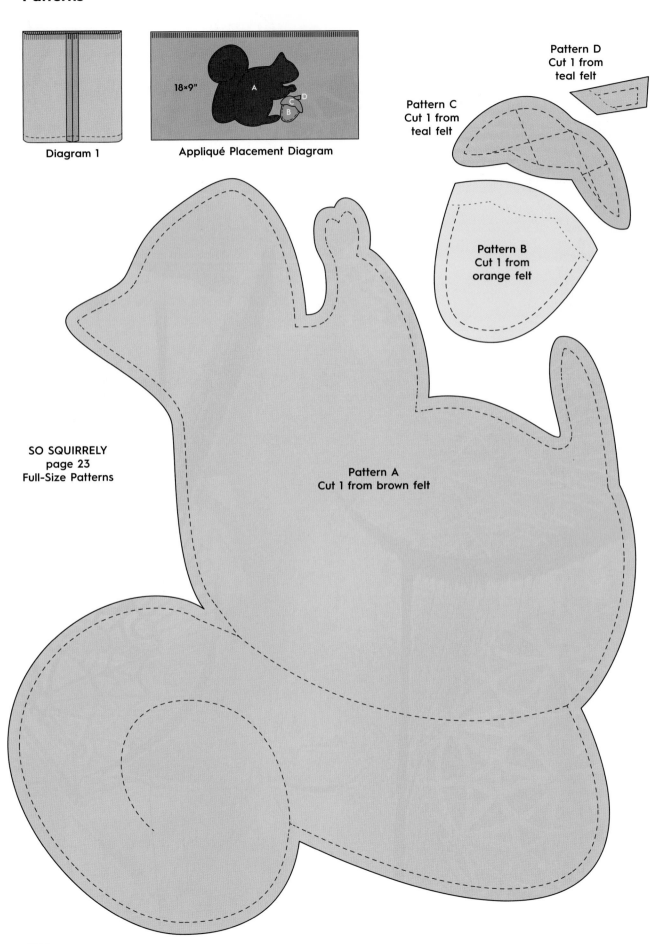

Diagram 1

18×9"

Appliqué Placement Diagram

Pattern D
Cut 1 from
teal felt

Pattern C
Cut 1 from
teal felt

Pattern B
Cut 1 from
orange felt

SO SQUIRRELY
page 23
Full-Size Patterns

Pattern A
Cut 1 from brown felt

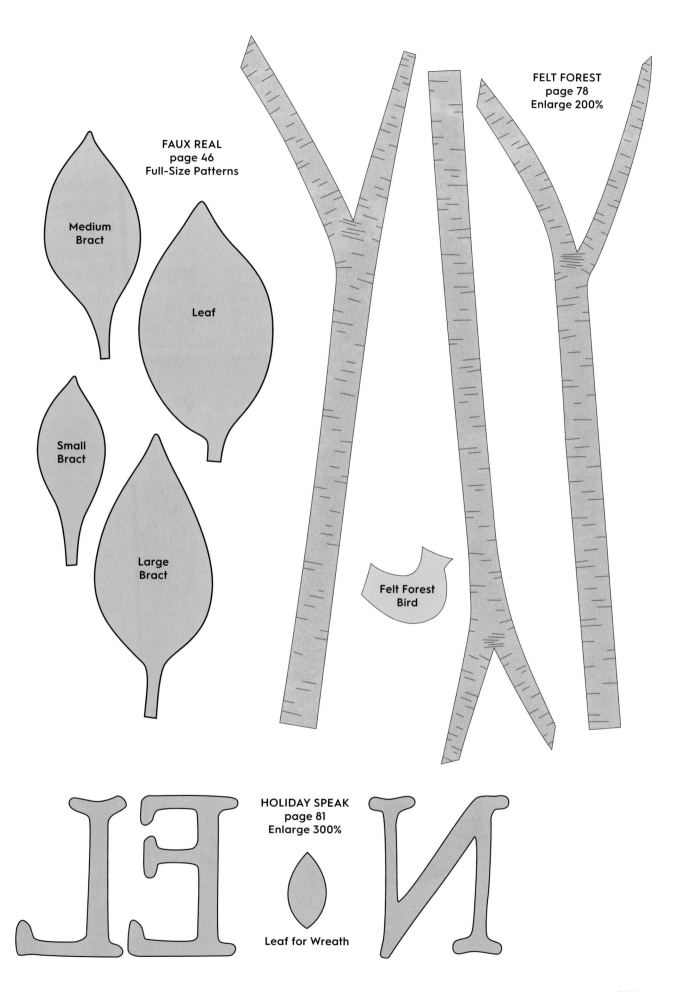

FAUX REAL
page 46
Full-Size Patterns

Medium Bract

Leaf

Small Bract

Large Bract

FELT FOREST
page 78
Enlarge 200%

Felt Forest Bird

HOLIDAY SPEAK
page 81
Enlarge 300%

Leaf for Wreath

Patterns

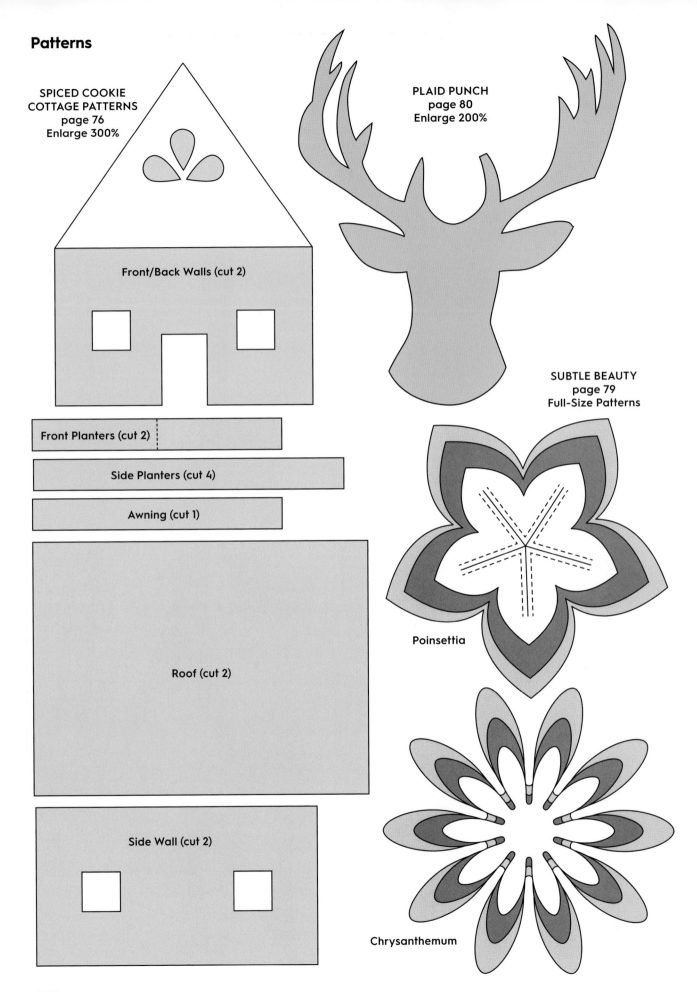

SPICED COOKIE
COTTAGE PATTERNS
page 76
Enlarge 300%

Front/Back Walls (cut 2)

Front Planters (cut 2)

Side Planters (cut 4)

Awning (cut 1)

Roof (cut 2)

Side Wall (cut 2)

PLAID PUNCH
page 80
Enlarge 200%

SUBTLE BEAUTY
page 79
Full-Size Patterns

Poinsettia

Chrysanthemum

SUITED FOR SANTA
page 66
Enlarge 200%

Patterns

CUSTOM
COASTERS
page 123
Enlarge 200%

TREE CUPCAKE
TOPPERS
page 151
Full-Size Pattern

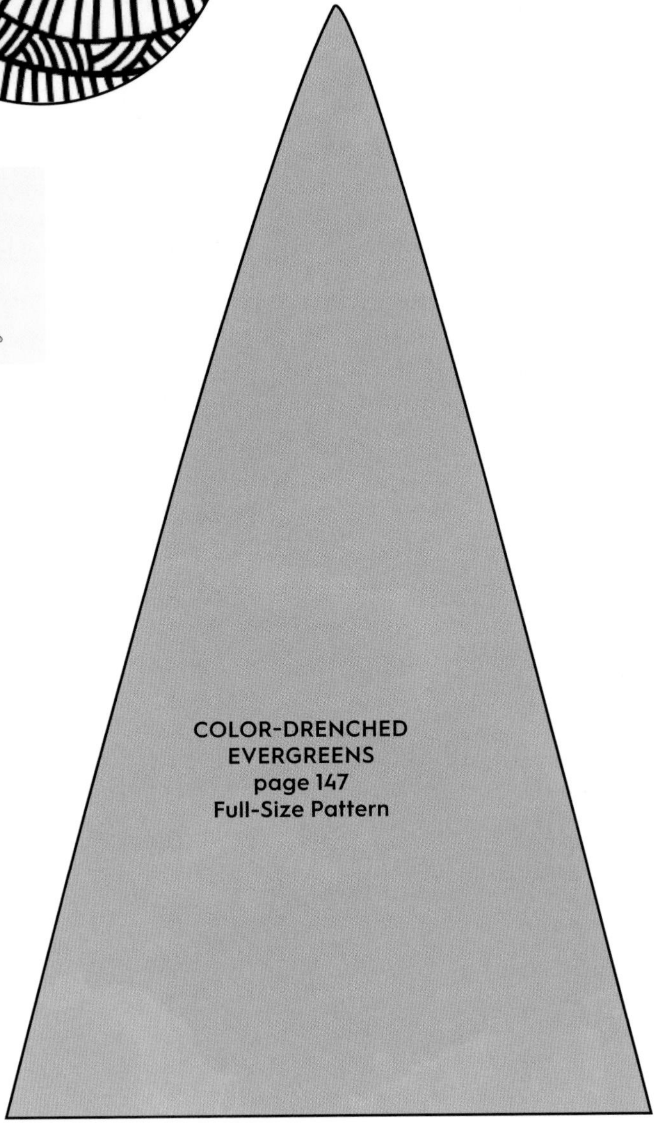

COLOR-DRENCHED
EVERGREENS
page 147
Full-Size Pattern

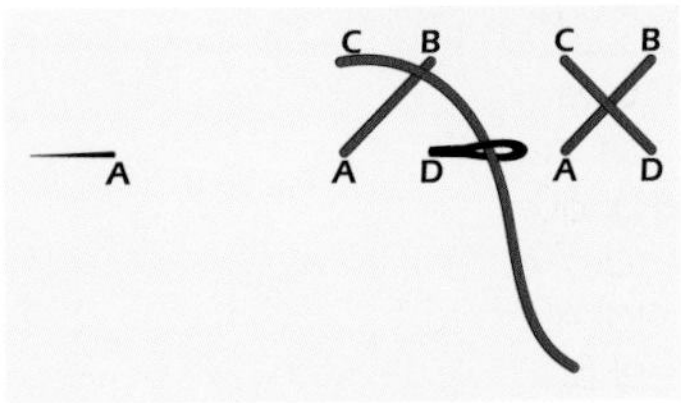

Cross-Stitch

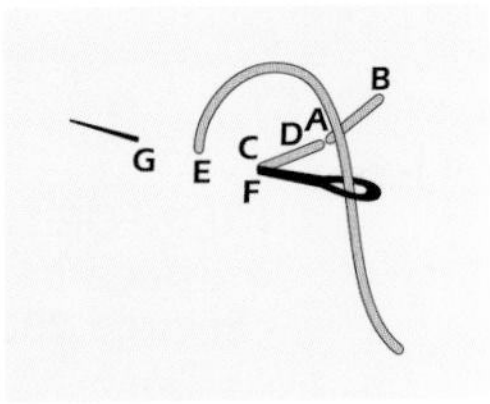

Backstitch

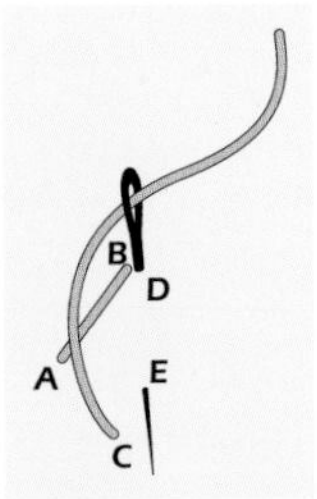

Straight Stitch

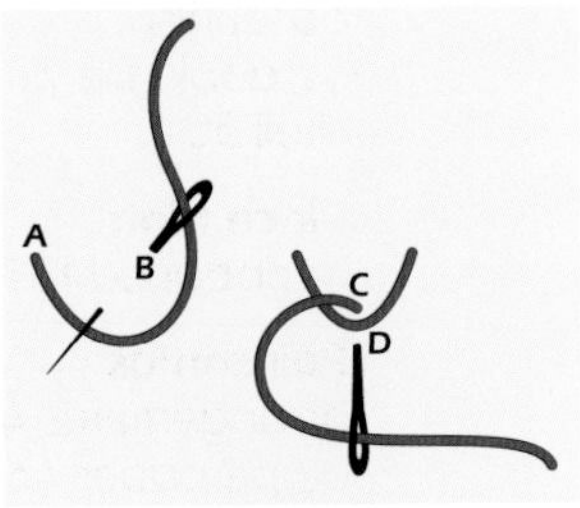

Fly Stitch

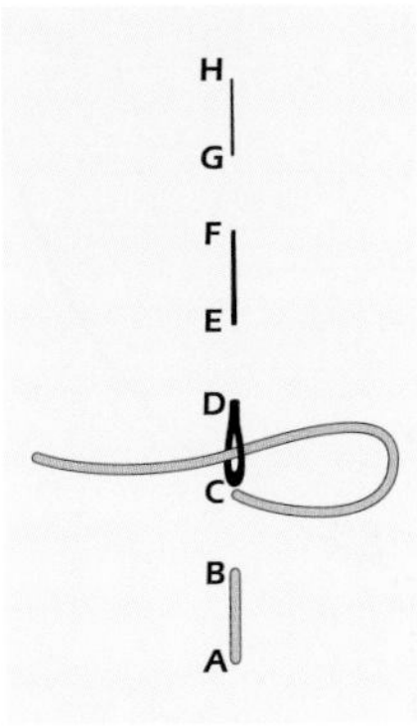

Running Stitch

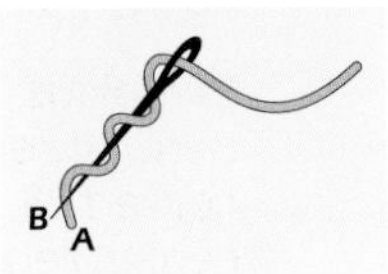

French Knot

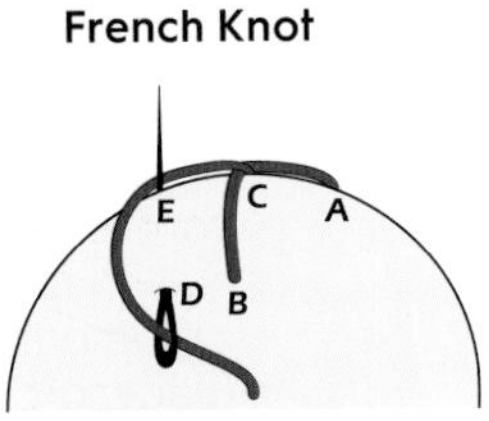

Blanket Stitch

index

CRAFTS AND DECORATING

Bead Projects
candle plate 142
cookie cutter trees 144
ornaments 145, 146
package initials 143
star tree topper 142

Bottles, Embellished 134

Bread Basket Liners 39

Candles
beribboned 9
inked 33

Candleholders & Plates
bead plate 142
cabbage-wrapped 33
glitter paper 87
house, paper 68
lace 32
metallic 30–31
pumpkin 32

Cardholders
clothespin 72
license plate 55

Centerpiece
bird with nest 72
candle and pumpkin 30–31, 32
license plate box 60–61
New Year's Eve carnation 83
poinsettia 47

Coasters
felt 42
jar lid 89
marking pen 122–123

Crayon Projects
snowman wall art 148–149
tree ornaments 146–147
wrapping paper and tag 148

Drinking Straw Projects
favor cups 150
greeting card 150
place card easels 150
snowflakes 151
tree cupcake toppers 151

Favors
coffee mug 41
crackers 85
lid 89
paper cup 8

Frames
poinsettia 46
polycarbonate 137

Gift Tags & Wraps
berry sprig 139
crayon wrapping paper
    & tag 148
drink coaster 138
initials 143
paper pom-pom 138
photo 136
pinecone 139
shell wreath 49
snowflake 139

Houses, Paper 63–65

Jars
bottles, embellished 134
buttoned up 129
burlap 126
gingerbread man trimmed 128
message 132–133
ribbon 127
snowman 130

License Plate Projects
box 61
card holder 55
key chain 58
napkin ring 56
ornament 60
star 59
stocking holder 54–55
vase 57

Metallic Projects
chair 25
lamp 24
mirror 26
vase 27

Mittens
bead ornament 145
utensil holder 38

Muddler 125

Napkin Ring
license plate 56
shell 50
veneer 17

New Year's Eve
candleholder 87
centerpiece 83
cracker favors 85
place cards 84
serving tray 86

tabletop 82–83

Ornament Holder 88

Ornaments
bead, melted 145
Christmas card 89
cookie cutter 36
felt twirler 75
license plate 60
package 67
pinecone star 71
pom-pom 69
shell 52
snowflake 151
snowman 88
tree 144, 146–147

Owls
pinecone 22

Photo Projects
frames 137
gift tags 136
vases 136

Pillows
birch tree 78
buck 80
floral 79
initial 42
noel 81

Place Cards
easel 150
Scrabble tile 73
shell 50

Place Mats
beribboned 10

Poinsettias
arrangements 47
crepe paper 46
frame 46
napkin rings 47
wall art 44–45

Pumpkins
beribboned 10
carved 28
centerpiece 31
under glass 29

Shell Projects
angel 49
candle holder 53
napkin ring 50
ornaments 52
placecard 50
serving dish 53

Index

tabletop tree 48
wreath 51
wreath, mini 49

Snowmen
light globe 40
pinecone 69
wall art, crayon 148-149

Stockings
faux fur cuffed 66
felt, stitched 74
oversized 37
plaid 72

Tablerunner
felt tree 38

Tabletops
New Year's Eve 82-83
Scrabble board runner 73

Tins 134

Trees
nature-trimmed 70
ornaments 144, 146-147
shell 48
tabletop 41

Trivets
squirrel 23

Vases
license plate 57
metallic 27
photo 136
wood wrapped 15

Wall Art
snowman 148-149
ribbon flowers 11

Wine Holder 124

Wood Veneer Projects
acorn 18
basket 14
fall letters 12-13
leaf, framed 12
mat 16
napkin ring 17
tray 19
vase 15

Wreaths
fox 20-21
hula hoop 43
nature 71
shell 51
skate 62
star 59

RECIPES

Appetizers
Apple-Cheddar Bites 119
Curried Potato Tarts 119
Easy Bake 118
No Cook 118
On a Stick 118

Buttermilk Pudding with Pomegranate Compote 105

Coffee, Cold Brew 135

Condiments, Sauces and Seasonings
Citrus Seasoning 131
Course Ground Mustard 132
Cranberry Mustard 132
Creole Mustard 132
Everyday Seasoning 131
Pacific Seasoning 131
Plum Compote 101
Prairie Seasoning 131
Salted Caramel 131

Cookies, Cakes, Bars
Chai-Spiced Pine Cones 109
Cherry-Hazelnut Crumb Bars 110
Chocolate-Pecan Coffee Cake 94
Cinnamon Roll Cookies 110
Mint-Ganache Sandwich Cookies 109
Pistachio-Cranberry Sticks 109
Vanilla Cookie Dough 108

Cranberry-Raspberry Spritz 93

Decorations
Spiced Cookie Cottage 76-77

Dips
Easy Bake 118
Mint Avocado Dip 119
Smoky Blue Cheese Dip 119
White Bean Hummus with Roasted Tomatoes 119

Eggs
Amaretto Brioche Bake 97
Bacon-and-Cheese Deviled Eggs 98
Breakfast Ham and Egg Cups 98

Everything Cracker Crisps 135

Flavored Butter
Bourbon-Vanilla Cookie 129
Gingerbread Cookie 126

Flavorings
Vanilla Coffee Creamer and variations 131
Vanilla Extract and variations 135

Herb-and-Garlic-Crusted Pork Roast 101

Sides
Arugula, Corn, and Tomato Salad with Ricotta Salata 94
Baby Potatoes Roasted in Salt 93
Caramelized Brussels Sprouts with Lemon 103
Cornmeal Spoon Bread 105
Double-Cheddar Holiday Biscuits 102
Macerated Grapefruit with Pistachios and Pomegranate 97
Roasted Broccoli and Olives 106
Scalloped Russet and Sweet Potatoes 103

Soups
All-American Cheeseburger Soup 113
Beef Stroganoff Soup 116
Chicken Enchilada Soup 116
Chicken Pot Pie Soup 114
Easy Taco Soup 112
Grilled Cheese Sandwich Soup 117
Lasagna Soup 113
Mac and Cheese Soup 117
Rich Beef Stew with Bacon and Plums 106
Spaghetti-Lover's Soup 115
Supreme Pizza Soup 115

CREDITS

Photo Styling
Sue Banker
Doug Samuelson

Photography
Marty Baldwin
Jason Donnelly
Carson Downing
Jacob Fox